America's Best Classrooms

America's Best Classrooms

How Award-Winning Teachers Are Shaping Our Children's Future

Daniel Seymour
Terry Seymour
and 30 Teachers of the Year

Peterson's Guides
Princeton, New Jersey

Library of Congress Cataloging-in-Publication Data

Seymour, Daniel, 1947–
    America's best classrooms : how award-winning
  teachers are shaping our children's future / Daniel
  Seymour, Terry Seymour.
       p.   cm.
  Includes bibliographical references.
  ISBN 1-56079-076-8
    1. Teaching. 2. Teachers—United States.
  I. Seymour, Terry, 1945– . II. Title.
  LB1025.3S49   1992
  371.1'02—dc20   91-40206

Composition and design by Peterson's Guides

Printed in the United States of America

10 9 8 7 6 5 4 3 2 1

To our award-winning parents,
Ray and Kate, who did a pretty decent job
of shaping their children's future.

1990–91 Teachers of the Year Who Contributed to This Book

Gloria V. Anderson—Sontag Elementary School, Rocky Mount, Virginia.

Mary K. Baker—RISE Learning Center, Indianapolis, Indiana.

Carolyn E. Baldwin—Emerson School, Bozeman, Montana.

Mercedes R. Bonner—Hodges Bend Middle School, Houston, Texas.

Jolanda M. Cannon—Wiley Ford Primary School, Wiley Ford, West Virginia.

Judith J. Crawford—Acequia Madre Elementary School, Santa Fe, New Mexico.

Leonard A. DeAngelis—Middletown High School, Middletown, Rhode Island.

James E. Ellingson—Probstfield Elementary School, Moorhead, Minnesota.

David S. Ely—Champlain Valley Union High School, Hinesburg, Vermont.

Barbara J. Firestone—McCollom Elementary School, Wichita, Kansas.

Roberta M. Ford—Eaglecrest Elementary School, Aurora, Colorado.

Nina D. Fue—Mary S. Shoemaker Elementary School, Woodstown, New Jersey.

Marilyn M. Grondel—Farr West Elementary School, Ogden, Utah.

Ann E. Haley-Oliphant—Kings Mills School, Kings Mills, Ohio.

Molly M. Hankins—Palmer Junior High School, Independence, Missouri.

Geraldine A. Hawes—Cleveland High School, Cleveland, Tennessee.

Pamela A. Johnson—Carpenter Elementary School, Monticello, Iowa.

Carole M. Kasen—Pinedale Elementary School, Rapid City, South Dakota.

Roderick D. Laird—Saratoga Elementary School/Middle School, Saratoga, Wyoming.

Bill D. Nave—River Valley School, Turner, Maine.

Anne P. Neidhardt—Broadneck Senior High School, Annapolis, Maryland.

Theresa Noonan—Gulf Breeze High School, Gulf Breeze, Florida.

Duane Obermier—Grand Island Senior High School, Grand Island, Nebraska.

John B. O'Connor—McKenzie Middle School, Watford City, North Dakota.

Barbara A. Prentiss—Smyth Road Elementary School, Manchester, New Hampshire.

Clemontene Rountree—Alice Deal Junior High School, Washington, D.C.

Lee Schmitt—Beaver Dam Junior High School, Beaver Dam, Wisconsin.

Howard R. Selekman—Dorseyville Junior High School, Pittsburgh, Pennsylvania.

Debbie Pace Silver—Keithville Elementary School, Keithville, Louisiana.

Charles Zezulka—Cutler Middle School, Mystic, Connecticut.

Contents

Preface

In 1990, more than 3,000 elementary and secondary school instructors were surveyed as to which of eight factors (among them education courses, in-service training, other teachers, and personal experience) contributed most to their abilities as teachers. In five of the seven teaching areas examined, the majority said their own experience and communication with other teachers were most important to their development. In comparison, other activities fared poorly in almost every teaching area.

After all the discussion in the past few years about teacher competence and the need to reform the way people are prepared for this vital profession—after the scores of reports in the past decade or so that focus on how little U.S. students know and how they can be educated more effectively—it comes as something of a shock to discover that almost 3,000 practicing teachers believe the best way to develop teaching skills is not through formal education courses but through teaching and talking to others who teach! Do we really need thousands of pages of statistical analysis to figure out how the education system can be improved? Do academic-generated hypotheses really get us anywhere? Why not go to the teachers and ask them about their classroom experiences? Why don't we learn from them and eliminate the middleman?

America's Best Classrooms draws extensively on the experiences of thirty of the country's 1990–91 Teachers of the Year to give an inside look at the profession and at the way individual teachers can and do make a difference.

Every year, one Teacher of the Year is chosen from each state, the District of Columbia, the Department of Defense Dependents Schools, and the U.S. territories. The selection process is rigorous: nominees must submit a candidate portfolio that contains background information, letters of recommendation, and essays addressing a set of topics designed to elicit their outlook on the profession (for example, "Describe your personal feelings and beliefs about teaching, including your conception of what makes an outstanding teacher."). Each of the states, the District of Columbia, and the territories chooses a single representative from the various nominees. The Council of Chief State School Officers, located in Washington, D.C., then convenes a national selection committee, and four finalists are picked from the fifty-plus representatives. From these four, the national Teacher of the Year is selected. Although there is only one national Teacher of the Year, the state winners serve as ambassadors for the teaching profession.

Through the fall of 1990, we contacted most of the 1990–91 Teachers of the Year to investigate what makes them stand out from their peers. We asked for and received copies of their candidate portfolios with nomination letters, references, and essays. Many shared speeches they had made recently. In some cases we did telephone interviews, while in others the teachers dictated responses to our questions onto audiotapes. We snooped and pried, queried and coaxed, all in an effort to get a grassroots perspective on the workings of the educational system, what's good about it, and how it might be improved.

These teachers' experiences form the basis for the seventeen chapters of this book. Some of their stories will make you laugh and others make you cry, but we hope all of them will give you cause to think. We are also well aware of the current volume of educational research, and, where appropriate, we refer to these studies and reports. Yet, when we found ourselves getting too far from the classroom or too overbearing in our approach, we inserted a cartoon from *Phi Delta Kappan* or a quirky anecdote. The overall effect is of a minestrone soup—the stock is based on what the best teachers think and do, to which is added some of this and that, a bit from here and a pinch from there. And we hope that readers find our mixture, like the soup, warming and healthful.

While *America's Best Classrooms* is written for anyone interested in the state of this country's education and the way some of the best teachers are rising to the challenge of shaping its children's future, we wrote the book with four specific groups in mind. First are the 3 million individuals who are currently teaching. Why? Because teachers are seekers. They are always looking for a way to reach one more confused child or inspire one more pupil to a new level of understanding.

A second group is composed of would-be teachers. These people will undergo intensive study of their majors and teaching methods in the years ahead. But they also will need a vision to guide them, a vision that can come from peering over the shoulders of some truly gifted teachers.

Then there are the administrators and school board members. The people who supervise school districts, high schools, middle schools, and elementary schools should be interested in creating the best possible classroom environments. Unfortunately, perfectly conceived classrooms cannot be bought or willed into existence. They evolve from the work of exceptional teachers and a system that knows how to support their efforts.

Finally, there are the parents. The more interest parents have in education and the more knowledgeable they become, the better the educational system will be. And if parents don't care about the nation's classrooms, their children will be the real losers.

The teachers you will meet in these pages are not perfect; they are people with the same hopes and concerns that most of us have. What sets them apart is their dedication—dedication not to an abstract ideal of education but to something much more tangible. They are dedicated to their jobs and to making sure they do the best they possibly can each and every day. And, more importantly, they are dedicated to the children, to helping them learn and helping them learn to live. We can only hope that everyone who reads this book shares in that dedication.

America's Best Classrooms would not have been possible without the support of Peter and Casey Hegener; the editing of Jim Gish, Sue Hesse, David and Janice Kaminsky, Owen O'Donnell, and Gisela Voss; the advice of Art Kuepper and Jim Buckley; and the understanding of Lynn Seymour, Tom Seymour, Jessica Seymour, and Jack Seymour. But most of all, it would not have been possible without the thirty Teachers of the Year who lent us their voices.

Thank you all.

Getting the Most Out of This Book

Everyone knows how to read a book: begin on page one, read each page from left to right until you run out of pages. This book is a bit different. We have dispensed with the niceties of building to a grand conclusion, page by page and chapter by chapter. We have ignored the standard of accumulating similar chapters into neat sections or parts. Instead, these chapters—or "nuggets," as we like to think of them—emerged from our discussions with Teachers of the Year. There is no specific order, no nugget is more important than another, and nothing is required reading (everything is optional). So we suggest you find a title that intrigues you or a quotation that delights you, and give the chapter a good reading. Skip around. Make notes in the margins. Do some underlining. Administer a few check marks or exclamation points if the mood strikes you. Have fun with it.

—D.S. and T.S.

Foreword

News item: Every year the U.S. school system graduates 700,000 young people who can't read their diplomas.

—*Fortune* (Spring 1990)

News item: We have a national dropout rate of 29 percent. As many as 60 percent of high school students drop out of some inner-city schools.

—*Forbes* (July 1990)

News item: American business spends $40-billion a year on education.

—*U.S. News & World Report* (March 1989)

How terrible are our schools? That depends on whom you listen to and what you read. Since the Bell Commission of 1983 described us as "a nation at risk" awash in a "rising tide of mediocrity," many people believe we should be operating in a crisis mode—issue everyone with a bucket and all start bailing. Others see room for improvement—lots of it—but without the frenzy. They counsel thoughtful change, reform, and cooperation rather than hysteria and finger-pointing. Still, at first glance, there is little doubt that the stories and statistics can be chilling.

We have all heard how disquietingly few schoolchildren can find the Atlantic Ocean on a map or discuss whether plants lean toward or away from the light. We have read reports of the studies that show Japanese and Korean kids computing mathematical rings around our kids. We are all too familiar with the headlines that scream, "Johnny's Miserable SATs"; the books that confide, "It's no secret that America's public schools are failing"; and the acid remarks of such individuals as former Secretary of Education William Bennett, who stated, "Our schools are among the worst in the civilized world." And then there are items like the following:

How Far We've Come

A CBS News report compared the top problems reported in public schools in the past (the 1940s) to those that are considered current reasons for concern.

Then	Now
1. Talking out of turn	1. Drug abuse
2. Chewing gum	2. Alcohol abuse
3. Making noise	3. Pregnancy
4. Running in halls	4. Suicide
5. Cutting in line	5. Rape
6. Robbery	6. Robbery
7. Littering	7. Assault

Source: CBS Evening News, February 9, 1987.

Exactly how terrible are our nation's schools? Not nearly as bad as they have been made to sound. The curricula in many school districts have undergone vast transformation, teacher education has improved across the board, more people than ever are receiving a high school diploma by studying for and passing the General Educational Development test (GED), and standardized test scores among minorities have risen in the past few years. Around the country, the next generation of Nobel Prize–winning physicists and chemists, bestselling authors, college and university professors, and business leaders is getting a solid start on its education.

Our schools—and, more important, our teachers—are like little boats being battered in the churning surf of commission reports and research studies. They are taking a fearful beating from each new wave of headlines, each new round of critics, detractors, and "experts" predicting the demise of the American classroom.

One organization, Project 30, has produced a report titled *The Reform of Teacher Education* that prescribes redesigning the way prospective teachers are educated. The Holmes Group, a consortium of more than 100 research universities, would reform not only teacher education but also the teaching profession, as described in their reports, *Tomorrow's Teachers* and *Tomorrow's Schools.* The National Endowment for the Humanities' report, *Tyrannical Machines,* has also advocated sweeping reforms. Its subtitle says it all: *A Report on Educational Practices and Our Best Hopes for Setting Them Right.*

The problem is that most plans for education reform in this country have followed a trickle-down pattern, in which legislators and theorists develop lofty goals with little input from the teachers who have to turn their ideals into reality. For example, in April 1991, President Bush unveiled an ambitious national plan called *America 2000: An Educational Strategy.* Calling for "a revolution in American education," this initiative is aimed at six educational goals proposed by the nation's governors. Briefly, these goals state that by the year 2000:

- All children in America will start school ready to learn.
- The high school graduation rate will increase to 90 percent.
- American students will leave grades 4, 8, and 12 having demonstrated competence in challenging subject matter.
- U.S. students will be first in the world in science and mathematics achievement.
- Every school in America will be free of drugs and violence.
- Every adult American will be literate.

Goal-setting is important. Having an agenda and strong, visible leadership is critical as well. Research that analyzes the options and discusses creative solutions to problems needs to continue at full speed. But, ultimately, the difference between success and failure depends on the people charged with actually making things happen. A football game is won or lost on the field by the players—not by the owners or fans, not by the coach and staff. A quality improvement plan in industry can detail what needs to be done to reduce defects, but the plan doesn't make improvement a foregone conclusion. Only the people on the production line can make it happen—not the CEO, not the stockholders, not the plant manager.

If school systems are to continue to improve, dropout rates continue to fall, and test scores continue to rise, it won't be because legislators and researchers would have it so. It will happen because of the teachers who must meet these challenges each and every day. It is their expertise, their enthusiasm and energy, their willingness to accept individual responsibility, that will make the difference. Our system of education will be able to respond to the pressures and demands placed on it only when teachers are thought of as part of the solution and not part of the problem.

Ann Haley-Oliphant, Ohio's Teacher of the Year, needs no reports and surveys to understand the ultimate goal of education reform and how to achieve it. "In schools across America," she said, "teachers must make miracles happen by grasping a spark of interest, a speck of talent, and a touch of wonder from students and producing an explosion of possibilities." You cannot legislate a miracle. No one has ever suggested that a commission report can generate a "touch of wonder," and many things may come out of the governor's office or the local school board, but an "explosion of possibilities" is not often one of them.

The fundamental reform that is needed in our education system cannot be directed or mandated from above. It cannot be researched, packaged, and distributed across the country like a vaccine. The change that is needed is rooted in the everyday lives of the teachers who are making learning come alive and spirits soar. In their classrooms is where our children's future is being shaped.

1

Kid People

"A genuine love for children, and respect for them, is what it's all about."
—Clemontene Rountree
Washington, D.C., Teacher of the Year

Why do people teach? Is it because of the tremendous salaries they earn? Is it because of the overwhelming respect and admiration they receive? Is it because they want a clean, quiet, comfortable place to work? Is it because of the liberal pension that allows them to retire to a condo in Palm Springs?

In *Profile of Teachers in the U.S.—1990*, published by the National Center for Education Information, about three fourths of those surveyed claimed a "desire to work with young people" as their main reason for becoming teachers. No other reason came close. And not only was the desire to work with young people a strong precondition for entering the profession, it is an even stronger reason for continuing to teach.

Marilyn Grondel, Utah Teacher of the Year, confirmed this when she told us, "I love to teach. I look forward to school starting each day. Teaching is not a job but involvement in children's lives.

"I remember how important my sixth-grade teacher made me feel," she recalled, "and I want my sixth graders to feel important and know how special they are. I remember the warmth and love from my summer kindergarten class, and I want that same warmth and love felt in my classroom.

"I feel excitement at the challenge of each new year, each new

Reasons for Being a Teacher

Question: What are the three main reasons you originally decided to become a teacher, and what are the three main reasons you are still teaching?

	Percent Originally	Currently
Desire to work with young people	70	78
Interest in subject matter	43	32
Value or significance of education to society	32	38
Never really considered anything else	28	9
Influence of a teacher in school	28	5
Long summer vacation	26	31
Influence of my family	24	5
Job security	19	32
One of the few professions open to me	11	5
Opportunity for a lifetime of growth	10	16
Sense of freedom in my own classroom	9	21
Preparation program in college appealed to me	8	*
Influence of a teacher or adviser in college	7	1
Financial rewards	4	7
Need for a second income in the family	4	15
Too much invested to leave now	1	30

Source: C. Emily Feistritzer, *Profile of Teachers in the U.S.—1990* (Washington, D.C.: National Center for Education Information, 1990), p. 48. Adapted and reprinted by permission.

"*E*ach child that spends time in my classroom is a gift to me from his or her parents. It is my responsibility to cherish that gift. "

day, and I want my students to feel the excitement and challenge of the learning process. I want to make a difference in the life of a child . . . . I love and respect children."

After pausing for a moment, she added, "Each child that spends time in my classroom is a gift to me from his or her parents. It is my responsibility to cherish that gift, to dream for that child, to lift him or her to new heights, and to help make the child the best he or she can be."

With such commitment, teaching becomes not just a job but an experience, not just a profession but a passion—what Nina Fue, New Jersey's Teacher of the Year, calls "the ride of your life." It's the challenge of fitting fifteen squirming kindergartners into snowsuits. It's actually enjoying the madly unpredictable behavior of 13-year-olds and appreciating the know-it-all smugness of high school seniors. It's connecting on a personal level with students and helping them attain clear, meaningful goals.

Herbert Kohl puts it nicely in *Growing Minds: On Becoming a Teacher:*

> The prime reason to teach is wanting to be with young people and help them grow. The long-term rewards of seeing your students become decent and creative adults are hard to understand at the beginning of a teaching career. Your major concern is getting through the year. After teaching a while, however, and remaining in contact with some of your graduates a while, you understand how important it can be for young people to have a teacher who cares

3

about their growth or introduces them to something that becomes of lifelong value to them.

What are the rewards of working with young people? The answer is not always obvious to the casual observer. Tracy Kidder observes in *Among Schoolchildren,* "Teachers usually have no way of knowing that they have made a difference in a child's life, even when they have made a dramatic one." There are, of course, exceptions—a smile or a touch, an unexpectedly perceptive question, an anonymous Valentine left on the corner of the desk, a look that says "I understand," a note from an appreciative parent, an unanticipated apology for some forgotten transgression, or a simple "thank you" from a small voice in the third row.

Consider this excerpt from a letter written in support of Roberta Ford's nomination for Colorado Teacher of the Year. Julie, a former student, wrote:

> No one ever forgets Mrs. Ford. For example, one day in class I looked back at the door and there was a young man dressed in a Navy uniform with his arms behind his back, standing tall and straight and looking very modest. Mrs. Ford looked back at him and her face was so happy. Her eyes got wide and her mouth dropped and she ran to him and they both started crying and hugging each other. That moment meant a lot to me—realizing that he once was a student of Mrs. Ford's and loved her as much as we all do.
>
> Thank you Mrs. Ford, I'll never forget you. Never.

Why do people teach? Nationwide surveys aren't needed to answer the question, nor are thick reports and detailed studies. Just sneak quietly into the back of Marilyn Grondel's or Nina Fue's classroom. Spend an hour or so at Eaglecrest School in Aurora, Colorado, with Roberta Ford and her eighth graders. The really good teachers, the ones who are shaping our children's future, are "kid people." In spite of kids' wisecracking, mud-tracking, nerve-racking ways, the great teachers just love young people. It's what makes their classrooms truly extraordinary places.

4

2

Turning Pebbles into Gold

*"Good teachers set high expectations for
students but make the steps for achieving
those levels clear and realistic."*

—**Pamela Adams Johnson**
Iowa Teacher of the Year

The 1990 National Governors Conference produced a series of
education goals that educators hailed as "ambitious": among
them, by the year 2000 all children in America will start school
ready to learn; by the year 2000 the high school graduation rate
will increase to at least 90 percent; by the year 2000 U.S. students
will be first in the world in mathematics and science achievement.
During the previous decade, numerous education reports, such as
A Nation at Risk, High School, and *A Place Called School,* featured bold
proposals, courageous recommendations, and lofty visions.

Duane Obermier, Nebraska Teacher of the Year, suggested to
us that the 1980s were the "Decade of Reports," the "Decade of
Talk," and went on to say he hoped the 1990s would become the
"Decade of Action and Implementation." Obermier's implication,
which we heard from many others as well, is that, while choosing a
destination and having goals are important, visions often degener-
ate into wishful rhetoric.

The problem is not a failure to think great thoughts on the
national level but a failure to engage these expectations within our
nation's classrooms. Let us give you an example from the 1988
movie *Stand and Deliver,* a portrait of Jaime Escalante, a mathemat-

We expect so little from kids. Is it really surprising when we get so little in return?

ics teacher in an East Los Angeles barrio school. In the film, Escalante, the school's principal, its mathematics department chairperson, and the rest of its math teachers are sitting around a conference table, and Escalante is speaking.

"I want to teach calculus next year."

The principal laughs. "Boy, that's a jump." More laughter.

"That's ridiculous," says the chairperson. "They haven't had trig or math analysis."

"They can take them both during the summer," Escalante responds.

"You expect our best students to go to summer school?"

"From 7 to 12 every day, including Saturdays. Yup. That'll do it."

The principal jumps back in. "You really think you can make this fly?"

Escalante stands his ground—"I teach calculus, or have a good day."

"Well, if this man can walk in here and dictate his own terms over my objections," says the department chairperson, "I see no reason for me to continue as chair. I'm thinking about those kids. If they try and don't succeed, you'll shatter what little self-confidence they have. These aren't the types that bounce back."

Anyone who has seen the movie or is familiar with Escalante's story knows that he went on to introduce the calculus course and achieve remarkable success. Hundreds of his barrio students have chalked up outstanding scores on the College Board Advanced Placement calculus test, gone to college, and pursued careers as doctors, civic and business leaders, professors, and, yes, teachers.

We expect so little from kids. Is it really surprising when we get so little in return? While governors are making headline-grabbing pronouncements about the importance of education, we are sending an entirely different message to students. In England and other industrialized countries, a typical school day is 8 hours long, and a school year is 220 days. In the United States, in contrast, the usual school day is 6 hours long, and the school year lasts a mere 180 days. We obviously operate at a considerably more leisurely pace. Then there is the curriculum. While the "Decade of Reports" bemoaned the lack of courses in literature, history, mathematics, and science, our schools are still loaded down with "social development" courses, such as home economics, sewing, and driver's education. Study halls, a euphemism for "day care," are used to round out the schedule for many of our schoolchildren.

When it comes to homework, Japanese children study an average of 16 hours a week in junior high school and 19 hours a week in high school. U.S. students, in contrast, spend 3 hours a week on homework in junior high and 4 hours a week in high school.

"I was a happy daytime viewer 'til education reared its ugly head."

Reprinted by permission of the artist.

If we don't challenge young people—if we don't stretch them—they will never see what they are capable of.

Taking into account the relative numbers of school days per year, some simple math brings us to the conclusion that U.S. high school students spend less than half the time studying in a year, whether in or out of school, than their Japanese peers!

This discrepancy *says* something about our expectations. The fact that U.S. kids spend up to four times as many hours in front of the television as they do in front of schoolwork at home *shouts* something about our expectations: They are too low.

The exceptional teachers we have come to know in the course of writing this book are probably not aware of national expectations. And it is doubtful that they could tell you how we compare to other countries in terms of homework. They have no control over the length of the school year, and, regrettably, many have no say over what the curriculum looks like either. They have reduced all of this down to their *own* expectation—*Everyone can learn.* Sure, children have varying capabilities. Just as some will never be professional basketball players no matter how many hours they practice their jump shot, others have no chance of becoming physicists or chemical engineers. But that's not the point. The crucial issue is that if we don't challenge young people—if we don't stretch them—they will never see what they are capable of.

In *Among Schoolchildren,* Tracy Kidder describes teacher Chris Zajac's thinking on this subject:

Children get dealt grossly unequal hands but that is all the more reason to treat them equally in school, Chris thought. "I think the cruelest form of prejudice is . . . if I ever said, 'Clarence is poor, so I'll expect less of him than Alice. Maybe he won't do what Alice does. But I want his best.'" She knew that precept wasn't as simple as it sounded. Treating children equally often means treating them very differently. But it also means bringing the same moral force to bear on all of them, saying, in effect, to Clarence that you matter as much as Alice and won't get away with not working, and to Alice that you won't be allowed to stay where you are either. She wanted Clarence to realize that he would pay a price for not doing his best and misbehaving. If she was consistent, Clarence might begin to reason that he could make school a lot easier by trying to do his work. If she got him to try, she could help him succeed, and maybe even help him to like school and schoolwork someday.

The notion that by expecting less of Clarence Chris would be practicing "the cruelest form of prejudice" is not just an admirable moral stand. The fact is that by *expecting less* from Clarence she would necessarily *get less* from Clarence. A teacher may form a poor opinion of a student based upon low standardized test scores, negative scuttlebutt in the teachers' room, a discouraging cumulative record, or the student's assignment to the "slow track." Regardless of its source, a teacher's low expectation results in that student's being treated differently.

Fascinating evidence for this conclusion can be found in research summarized by Jere Brophy and cited in *NEA Today* . The research shows that teachers tend to

- demand less from the students of whom they have low expectations ("lows") than from those of whom they have high expectations ("highs")
- give "lows" less time to answer questions
- give "lows" the answer or call on someone else rather than try to improve the "lows'" response by repeating the question, providing clues, or asking a new question
- seat "lows" farther away from them than "highs"
- accept more low-quality or incorrect responses from "lows"

- give briefer, less informative responses to the questions of "lows" than to those of "highs"

- call on "lows" less often than "highs"

- pay less attention to "lows" and interact with them less frequently

- praise "lows" less frequently than "highs" for their successes

Good teachers work hard to overcome the natural tendency to expect less of their Clarences. They don't take the easy way out. They push kids, *all of them,* to do their very best and improve their performance. It's tough work to believe that the Clarences can make it, especially when the Clarences don't believe it themselves. But the best teachers willingly accept the burden.

This reminds us of the story of a fellow who was hiking alone on a rugged mountain trail. At one point on the trail, he noticed a sign that read, "Pick up some pebbles from the pile at the base of this sign. Put them in your pocket. At the end of the day, you will be both glad and sad." The hiker looked at the pile of pebbles, chose two of the smallest, and put them into his pocket. As he was about to go to sleep that night, he remembered the pebbles and, removing them from his pocket, found they had turned to gold. He was very glad he had picked them up, and he was very sad that he hadn't picked up more and bigger pebbles.

Too many of our nation's teachers focus their energies on the pebbles that are easiest to carry. But others, such as North Dakota's John O'Connor, refuse to settle for the smaller reward. He told us in no uncertain terms, "My job is to identify what students' abilities are—*no matter what they've been told they are.*" He added, "Once I identify what they're *really* capable of, I push, I pull . . . I praise them, almost embarrassingly, for having worked up to their abilities." His classroom, like Pamela Johnson's and Duane Obermier's, is a place for reaching and stretching. It is a place for dreaming—then doing. After all, why be in the small-pebble business when you can be working with chunks of gold?

Aim So High You'll Never Be Bored

*The
greatest waste
of our
natural resources
is the
number of people
who never
achieve their
potential.
Get out
of that
slow lane.
Shift
into that
fast lane.
If you think
you can't,
you won't.
If you think
you can,
there's a
good chance
you will.
Even making
the effort
will make
you feel
like a new
person.
Reputations
are made
by searching
for things that
can't be done
and doing them.
Aim low:
boring.
Aim high:
soaring.*

Copyright © 1986 by United Technologies Corporation.

3

Mr. and Mrs. Cleaver,
Where Are You?

*"The most pertinent issue in education
today is lack of parent involvement in the
education of their children."*
—**Mary Kay Baker**
Indiana Teacher of the Year

The National PTA Talks to Parents begins with the statement "The difference between a good school and a great school is the parents." And the research backs up its contention 100 percent. In *The Evidence Continues to Grow: Parental Involvement Improves Student Achievement*, Anne Henderson summarizes the results of nearly fifty studies of parental involvement and concludes:

> Programs designed with strong parent involvement produce students who perform better than otherwise identical programs that do not involve parents as thoroughly, or that do not involve them at all. Schools that relate well to their communities have student bodies that outperform other schools. Children whose parents help them at home and stay in touch with the school score higher than children of similar aptitude and family background whose parents are not involved. Schools where children are failing improve dramatically when parents are called in to help.

To make this unanimous, we can throw in the opinion of teachers as well. A recent *New York Times* article on education states that

═══ **Going to the Source** ═══

Years ago, someone gave one of the authors the following poem. It contains great wisdom that is now passed on to you. Guard it well.

> *The college professor says:*
> *Such rawness in a pupil is a shame,*
> *Lack of preparation in high school is to blame.*
> *But the high school teacher says:*
> *Good heavens! Such crudity; the boy's a fool.*
> *The fault, of course, is in the middle school.*
> *But the middle school teacher says:*
> *From such stupidity may I be spared,*
> *They send them to me so unprepared.*
> *But the primary teacher says:*
> *Kindergarten blockheads, and they call*
> *that preparation? Worse than none at all.*
> *But the kindergarten teacher says:*
> *Such a lack of training never did I see.*
> *What kind of mother must that mother be?*
> *But the mother has the final word. Mother says:*
> *Poor helpless child; he's not to blame.*
> *His father's people are all the same.*

"In surveys, teachers say the lack of parent involvement is more damaging to education than a lack of money for the schools or a lack of discipline among students."

Moreover, it should come as no surprise that our Teachers of the Year have powerful opinions concerning the influence of parents. New Hampshire's Barbara Prentiss told us how her father, "the son of immigrant parents and one of nine children, instilled in me from a very early age the importance of education. Although tired from his struggling law practice, he would take the time to read to me. As I grew older, my dad helped me with school assignments, especially history and geography, which he made come alive through storytelling. I acquired his passion for learning."

Mercedes Bonner of Texas described "the teacher whose teaching and learning style impressed me most—my mother, Rebecca Green Russell. Even though she only had a high school education, my mother was 'educated' through her interest in people, books, and numerous hobbies. It always amazed me to hear people ask if my mother was a teacher after they met her. She was well-read, articulate, and opinionated and revealed, in the words of Kipling, an 'insatiable curiosity.'"

Missouri's Molly Hankins "was blessed with patient parents. Although both worked full-time in the family business, they always nurtured my creativity and stressed the importance of learning. Daddy was apologetic about his eighth-grade education, and I think one of his proudest moments was seeing his daughter graduate from college, certified to teach."

Given the often strident national debate on education, it is encouraging that everyone is able to agree on something: parents who show a positive attitude toward learning significantly increase their children's achievement. The influence appears to be strongest when children are young and their parents talk, listen, and read to them, but it continues into middle school and high school. In fact, students achieve more when their parents simply take an interest in what they do in school.

With so much evidence available, so much commonsense material, you would expect both the quality and quantity of school-family interactions to increase greatly. Teachers should have realized that they cannot succeed alone. Parents should have understood that their responsibilities to their children extend beyond providing food and shelter. The relationship between parents and teachers should be a power-sharing coalition, a mutual admiration society. This hasn't happened, for several sad reasons.

On the parenting side, there is "affluenza," a disease of the well-to-do. It is a curious affliction that generates uncontrollable fits of self-centeredness. It manifests itself in family vacations to the Caribbean in the middle of the school year or weeknight trips to

In the 1990 version, June and Ward Cleaver are divorced, and June is raising Wally and the Beave by herself.

the Ice Capades at the expense of homework. The parent-teacher interactions that do occur tend to focus on problems: "What do you mean my Johnny got a D? He's no D student. Where did you get your degree from anyway? So he missed some homework assignments. I'm going straight to the superintendent about this. Don't you know that my taxes pay your salary?" It's a little like the owners blaming the BMW mechanic for the $2000 repair bill when they neglected to change the oil.

Then there are the problems of Middle America, with nearly one child in four under the age of 18 living with a single parent and only 7 percent of school-age children living in a two-parent household with only one wage earner. Over 70 percent of the mothers of school-age children work outside the home. In the 1990 version, June and Ward Cleaver are divorced, and June is raising Wally and the Beave by herself. She works a shift at the CVS pharmacy in order to pay the mortgage and supplement Ward's child-support payments. Wally and Beaver hang out with Eddie Haskell at the mall until 9 just about every night and then hide the negative progress reports their teachers send home.

To get a picture of parenting on the bottom rung of the socio-economic ladder, you can take the statistics for Middle America and double them. According to Bureau of the Census reports, 54 percent of African-American children and 30 percent of Hispanic children live in single-parent homes. Research has shown that the single-parent family is a major contributor to kids' dropping out of school. Add to that five others—a family income under $15,000, no one at home, uneducated parents, a sibling who dropped out, and limited English proficiency—and you begin to get the picture of what these parents are up against.

We are not talking here about parents who must choose between going to their aerobics class or attending a PTA meeting. We are not even talking about Ward Cleaver bowing out of going to a school open house with June because he has to work late. We are talking about people so overwhelmed with the daily struggle to survive that good parenting skills sometimes fall by the wayside. In school after school, as in the example on the next page, teachers grapple with the results.

While it's easy to see parents as the source of the problem, there is also reason to believe that some teachers make interested parents feel like intruders. They erect barriers that say, in effect, "I am

"Remember, Ruthann, excel!"

Reprinted by permission of the artist.

the professional here. Thanks for coming, really. Can't wait to see you again at the next open house in spring 1993." Others simply don't want to add hours of "extra" phone calls and conferences to their schedules. Some teachers have had bad experiences with intrusive parents. Still others see the value of parent-teacher interaction and are willing to go the extra distance to make it happen but are continually beaten down by the administrative hassles in-

═ I Heard from Only One ═

In September 1988, Emily Sachar took a one-year leave of absence from her position as a New York Newsday *reporter to teach eighth-grade mathematics at IS 246, the Walt Whitman Intermediate School in the Flatbush section of Brooklyn. Upon returning to the newspaper, she wrote a series of articles about her experiences.*

For the first pair of open houses in November, I bought chocolates, drew up a sign-in list, and had puzzles on hand, like those I was using in my math classes. But parents of only one-third of my 151 students showed up, even though they had to come to retrieve their children's first quarter report cards.

I also encouraged parents to attend PTA meetings. The Whitman PTA had 30 members, and no more than 19 people showed up for the routine meetings. Whitman had more than 1,700 students.

And, I often offered to cut short my lunch hour or to surrender my coveted preparation periods to meet with parents whose children were having a hard time in school. But, while some parents showed for scheduled appointments at the Flatbush, Brooklyn, school, most did not. Two months into the school year, I sent letters to the parents of 19 students whom I intended to fail for the first marking period. I heard from only one.

Source: Emily Sachar, "My Life as a Teacher—The Best of Times, the Worst of Times" (New York: *New York Newsday* Special Edition, January 1990), p. 21. Reprinted by permission.

"Creating parent-teacher partnerships is beneficial to all."

volved—thirty-five teachers and only one telephone, no budget for mailing out a newsletter, and so on.

In spite of the many barriers to closer school-parent relationships, many good schools and all good teachers make an extra effort to generate active involvement. Len DeAngelis, Rhode Island's Teacher of the Year, comes at the issue from a perspective of shared responsibility, suggesting to us that "Parents who begin to sense some ownership in the schools become partners with the school in accomplishing its missions."

Teachers like Len are creative in finding ways of reducing the distance between home and school. They give homework assignments that involve the family. They arrange for report cards and school reports to be sent to both custodial and noncustodial parents. They give parents a course synopsis that includes homework expectations and grading criteria. They get parents to help in planning and presenting career days. They hold workshops for parents on helping their children master specific skills. They see themselves as conspirators with parents in educating their kids. Or as DeAngelis went on to say, "Creating parent-teacher partnerships is beneficial to all, since it fosters collaboration, cooperation, and allegiance to a common goal and an understanding of the educational process."

If parents can't find time to get to school, then, as West Virginia's Jolanda Cannon suggests, it's every teacher's responsibility to "step from behind the classroom door." Any and every way to get parents "plugged in" must be pursued, including the use of modern technology, if need be.

Picture a parent calling her daughter's school at 6 p.m. on a

Tuesday evening. Ring. Click. "Hello! Thank you for calling the Springfield School Parent Information Hotline. Please enter your two-digit class number to receive information from your child's teacher at any time during this message."

Beep. Beep. "Hi there. This is Lynn Seymour. For the spelling assignment that's due tomorrow, parents give a pretest tonight. Please check spelling sentences. In reading, we're studying the pyramids. You might ask your child why the pyramids were built and in what country most of them are located."

About forty schools in a dozen states are experimenting with just such a 24-hour call-in system, developed by Advanced Voice Technologies of Nashville, Tennessee, and underwritten by the Pacific Telesis and Wells Fargo foundations. The system makes it easy for a teacher to "connect" with hundreds of parents each day. It also enables parents to avoid the nightly quiz: "What did you do in school today?" "Got any homework?" By pressing other numbers on the menu, parents can listen to a calendar update, PTA information, and a monthly message from the principal.

Teachers cannot continue to blame parents and society for the poor performance of students. Pointing fingers doesn't solve problems. If children fail, it's not solely the fault of their parents' failed marriage. It's not society's fault that economic conditions require both parents to work. Nor is it practical to ignore the problems that land on teachers' doorsteps every September. It is tiresome and dispiriting to be forever playing Mr. or Ms. Fix-It, constantly trying to catch up.

Teachers cannot succeed alone. The odds are far too heavily stacked against them. They need allies, partners, and collaborators, because education is too important to be left to the schools alone.

4

Heinz 57

"For far too long, we have been trying to teach students as if they were all alike."
—Barbara Prentiss
New Hampshire Teacher of the Year

Education is a sorting process, often beginning with a tracking procedure that separates the slow from the fast learners with such tags as "red birds" and "blue birds" or "special ed" and "regular ed." Programs in English as a second language achieve another kind of sorting. Further on, students are categorized by destination—college preparatory or vocational-technical.

At the college level, students choose a major by the end of their sophomore year, after which most of their time at school is spent interacting with people with similar interests, whether mathematics or English or biology. A college education, therefore, creates homogeneous groupings of subject-centered individuals. It's a subtle process, years in the forming, and it's hard to realize the exceptional extent to which our educational system separates us from each other and from the differences between us.

In such careers as computer software engineering or accounting, a narrow focus is probably useful, since most of one's colleagues will be engineers or accountants, and the need to keep up with constant technical advances tends to force specialization. But how about elementary school teachers or high school English teachers? They are educated in much the same manner as these other professionals, but, once they earn their diplomas, they are thrown back into a classroom world that bears no resemblance to the classrooms they have known in the course of their own education.

Increasing diversity—not homogeneity—is what's happening in America's classrooms in the 1990s. As a pluralistic democracy composed of many minorities, our mission is to attempt to educate *everyone*—the economically disadvantaged, the physically challenged, the learning disabled, the non–English speakers, the children of dysfunctional families.

While the strengths that derive from ethnic diversity should be evident to everyone, the fact is that a new teacher in certain metropolitan-area schools may be in for a bit of a culture shock. Cultural mosaics and living tapestries are all very well, but that is of scant comfort to a new teacher unfamiliar with not only the languages but the cultural norms of the assorted ethnic, racial, and religious groups in the class. For instance, a pat on the head of a Chinese

══════ Latin May Be ══════ Dead, . . .

but all of the following languages were spoken among the 654 students attending Oakridge Elementary School in Arlington, Virginia, in 1989.

Amharic	Portuguese
Arabic	Somali
Bengali	Spanish
Chinese	Tagalog
Ga	Thai
Japanese	Tigrinya
Khmer	Twi
Korean	Urdu
Nyanja	Vietnamese
Persian	

Source: NEA Today, December 1989, p. 4. Reprinted by permission.

*T*he teacher of today and tomorrow is unlikely to face a class that fits any stereotype.

child is an insult. Jehovah's Witnesses don't celebrate birthdays or holidays and don't salute the flag. Muslim children fast from dawn to sunset every day during Ramadan, the ninth month of the Islamic calendar. Are our teachers prepared to respond to this diversity with sensitivity?

In *Among Schoolchildren,* Tracy Kidder describes his year spent observing teacher Chris Zagac's fifth-grade class. Among her students are Pedro and Judith. Pedro has been raised by his grandmother and has six half-brothers, each of whom has a different mother. He comes to class one day and misses two. When he is present, he falls asleep. Pedro is struggling constantly to overcome the terrible odds that he faces. In complete contrast, Judith comes from a stable traditional family and is the darling of the class.

When asked on a social studies test to define Tory and identify John Adams, Pedro manages only "Tory. Like a grup of sogrs." After puzzling out Pedro's phonetic rendition of "group of soldiers," Zagac comes to Judith's response: "Tory. A person that didn't think we should breakaway from England. John Adams. A fellow patriot that was one of the Sons of Liberty. He was the second president of the United States. He was one of the Signers of the Declaration of Independence. He was one of the Representatives of the United States with France. He helped fight the Revolutionary War."

Every classroom will have its Judiths and Pedros. The teacher of today and tomorrow is unlikely to face a class that fits any stereotype—as with Heinz, there are 57 varieties. Whether it's Philadelphia or Los Angeles or smaller towns like Eugene, Oregon, and

Ilion, New York, the notion of an average student has less and less relevance. And chances are the new teachers facing this international ark of children will be predominantly white and female and holders of a bachelor's degree in education, a homogeneous, subject-centered group of people much like our computer software engineers and accountants.

How are we dealing with the diversity that fills our nation's classrooms? One thing we *continue* to do is use tracking. The idea has been that if we can divide students into more uniform groups it will be easier to teach them and easier for them to learn. John Goodlad, in his book *Teachers for Our Nation's Schools,* says that the grouping of children in the primary grades into low, medium, and high groups—particularly for reading and arithmetic—is as "alive and well today as it was 50 years ago." He goes on to comment that "the emergence of an impressive body of research showing that such practices not only exacerbate the spread of individual differences, further disadvantaging the lowest groups, but also deter individual diagnosis and remediation has not influenced these practices one whit."

Another way we are responding to student diversity is by simply ignoring it. At the beginning of this century, Ford Motor Company was successful with its Model T, the first mass-produced automobile. It came in one color—black. As other companies began producing cars of other colors, Ford remained resolute in selling what it wanted to sell—black cars. This example is used in all introductory marketing textbooks to distinguish between selling and marketing: marketing is driven by the needs of the consumer, while selling involves producing a product according to internal desires and standards and, for all practical purposes, ignoring individual differences.

By *ignoring* individual differences in education, the system tends to gravitate toward a Model T approach. Teachers are issued a textbook and a curriculum and are expected to generate lesson plans based on these. The objective is to cover the material and pass students on to the next level of textbook/curriculum/lesson

We have been offering not an education for children but, instead, an education that we do to children.

plan. This is teaching to the middle, to the average, while ignoring different learning styles and rates of development. The process is built around subject matter and the simple-minded need to cover the material. It is not an education *for* children but, instead, an education that we do *to* children.

Many of our Teachers of the Year discussed a more positive way of responding to the diversity in America's classrooms. It is the way of the marketers, not the sellers. It celebrates differences and adapts and extends teaching styles to harmonize with students' backgrounds, learning styles, and learning rates. It is much more student centered, especially in the lower grades, than it is subject centered.

Barbara Prentiss, New Hampshire's Teacher of the Year, expressed it well: "We have put them in tracks, grouped them, and tried to organize them and cluster them in one way or another. I think we need to personalize learning. We need to become aware of different rates of learning and try to get rid of time schedules." In this approach, which is flexible and student directed, "our responsibility is to look for ways of altering what we are teaching, and how we are trying to teach it, to meet the needs of a particular child." No hint of tracking here, no suggestion that the most you can hope for is that 50 percent of the class will "get it."

South Dakota, where Carole Kasen was voted Teacher of the Year, has the largest Native American population in the country. It also has its newly arrived immigrant groups and its conservative ranching community. With such diversity, it comes as no surprise that "wherever we try to diverge from the curriculum and work for

25

the child instead of whatever the administrative mandates are, we run into trouble." And yet, as with all of America's best teachers, Kasen knows what really comes first: "From my personal standpoint, I'm looking at the children, and the heck with the programs. . . . We need to take a look at what the kids need," she continued. "There is no such thing as a homogeneous group of kids. All classes are different. All kids are different."

Perhaps no one expressed the appreciation of the differences between children better than Duane Obermier, Nebraska's Teacher of the Year, in a recent speech to new teachers: "As your teaching careers unfold, you can look forward to limitless challenges and a fascinating array of students." Below is his description of just a few who have passed through his classroom.

Alan, Bill, Lynette, and Jane

Perhaps you'll have an Alan. This brilliant student was in the top ten of a 400-member senior class last year: he mastered a difficult desktop publishing computer program used with our student newspaper, he had leading roles in plays, and he did all this with an easygoing sense of humor that always made me glad he was around. Perhaps you'll have a Bill. Bill failed my speech class two years ago and wanted to quit school. He didn't quit, and, with his limited academic skills, minimal family support, and being almost on his own financially, we were surprised when he returned to school a year ago. Classes went poorly for him again, and last year he did quit. As far as I know, he's now in the Job Corps. Perhaps you'll have a Lynette. Goal oriented, businesslike, efficient, reliable, meticulous, she was a top-notch yearbook staff member last year. Her senior English teacher predicted to me that Lynette would produce the best senior research paper out of his students, and he assured me later that she did. Perhaps you'll have a Jane. During the year, Jane threatened suicide, lived in a shelter home, and yet worked hard to produce acceptable work in my class.

It is evident from their words that the teachers we talked with have managed to overcome their own homogeneous, subject-centered education. They don't ignore individual differences and don't try to "group" them away. They don't try to sell a standardized, lockstep curriculum to a classroom wonderfully full of all 57 varieties but seek to diversify their approach to teaching based upon the requirements of their students—the Lynettes and Bills, the Janes and Alans. Responding to needs is their angle; working for individual improvement is their game.

5

Did You Hear the One About . . . ?

"It takes an indefatigable sense of humor. . . ."
—Roberta Ford
Colorado Teacher of the Year

Roberta Ford must be short, or why would a bunch of eighth graders come into her class on their knees, singing "Short People"? Why would one of the students ask classmates to "Check the bottom of your shoes, Mrs. Ford is missing!" Short in stature, perhaps, but she must have a big sense of humor and sizable self-confidence. "It takes," she says, "a strong sense of self so that you're not threatened by the crazy things students do or say as they try to figure out who they are and where they're going."

One of the best signs of a good classroom is laughter. Sure, education is a serious business, but it doesn't have to be solemn. Grim-faced teachers presiding over neatly arranged rows of unsmiling kids sitting hands folded, upright, unsquirming, and noiseless may be peaceful. It may be quiet. It may be organized. The principal may even like it that way, because it looks so neat and efficient. But it's not natural. Put twenty or thirty young people in a room together and, if it isn't a detention hall or a Mass, every once in a while there ought to be a good, healthy round of guffaws and giggles.

Debbie Pace Silver is a rapid-talking dynamo who teaches

"*P*uberty is one of the funniest things. A student may act different from one day to the next. "

eighth-grade science in rural Louisiana. A former theater arts major with twenty years of teaching experience, she says unashamedly, "I'm a ham, and I'll try almost anything to get my students to understand." A lesson on inertia finds her zipping around the room on roller skates and occasionally slamming into lab tables. A discussion about mass leads to observations on her weight. When the kids have a problem understanding the scientific method, Johnny appears. He is a rather slow student, one of Silver's several alter egos, who stuns the class with his lack of understanding and outrageous assumptions. By straightening Johnny out, the kids come to grips with the essentials of the lesson. But this is not humor for its own sake—Silver consciously uses humor to help students learn. All her lessons are carefully planned and orchestrated.

The first several days of classes are spent clearly defining her expectations, the rules of behavior, and the consequences of messing up. But even this is done with humor. She acts out unacceptable behavior, uncannily mirroring all the quirks of the typical adolescent. The kids know exactly what she's talking about. "Puberty is one of the funniest things," she says. "A student may act different from one day to the next. It's tough. I tell them the things expected of me and the things I expect from them."

Silver, who fell into teaching by accident, didn't always teach this way. Early on, for fear of losing control of her classes, she suppressed her true personality and "acted" the stern, dour type. Increasingly frustrated by this deception, she realized she either would have to leave teaching or let the "ham" out. Luckily for her students, she decided to stay. The lesson she learned is valuable to all new teachers—teachers are most effective when they reconcile their pedagogy with their personality.

"Teaching is not hard when you align your personal philosophy and style with the pedagogic skills that you use in your classroom," she says. Which means that what Debbie Pace Silver does in her classroom may not be the best approach for all teachers. Each needs to find an appropriate alignment.

One of the key ingredients of humor is spontaneity. Beginning teachers often think that they must be the primary source of the humor—they must furnish the routines, the punchlines, the anecdotes. Frankly, there is something to this, because establishing control is important, even control of the humor. As time passes, however, and the teacher feels more confident and comfortable with the students, and standards of behavior and respect have been established clearly, "letting it happen" can be an unlimited source of fun.

Colorado's Roberta Ford clearly understands another value of laughter. It can be effective in putting students at ease with their own self-doubts. If she is comfortable with her short stature and can treat it lightly, kids in her classes should be better able to handle their own insecurities (which, with eighth graders, can change hourly with earth-shattering magnitude). It's very important that teachers laugh at themselves with their students. Blunders and screw-ups are part of life. Good teachers recognize that a mispronounced word, a pratfall, or a bad day can, when treated casually and with a smile, become valuable learning experiences. As Maryland's Anne Neidhardt says, "The message goes out to the students that it's okay for them to mess up sometimes, because they're going to be able to recover and go on from there."

Recently one of the authors attended a theater workshop with a group of middle school children. During a presentation on costuming, the instructor invited the students to try on some of the costumes she had been talking about. A few of the braver, more outgoing kids dove in, tripping over themselves to get at the plastic chain mail, the capes, the Civil War costumes. But most of the kids held back, timid, not sure if the potential fun was worth the risk of embarrassment. In charged one of their teachers, eagerly pulling

The Little Engine That Did

Herbert Kohl has written about how he learned the value of spontaneity and of controlling his teacher's ego. He had spent the summer planning lessons for a fifth-grade social studies unit on the Industrial Revolution.

My idea was to demonstrate a simple version of a working factory to my class and then build a large, fairly accurate scale model of a cotton mill while studying the psychological, social, and economic effects of industrialization. Sometime during the first week of school I brought in the steam engine and a simple piston press that was powered by the engine. I was proud of my teaching plans and sure my students would be excited by them. One of the students filled the engine with water and another lit the can of Sterno under the boiler. As the water began to heat, we could hear sputtering and rumbling inside the engine, and a bit of steam escaped through the safety valve. Suddenly a voice in the back of the room proclaimed, "It's farting," and everyone started laughing and holding their noses. I was shattered, my face became red; my wonderful ideas had been turned into nothing but a joke. I blew out the fire, put the engine away, and insisted that everyone get out their workbooks and do an extra assignment. It took me several days to recover my confidence to do something interesting again and try to get my students out of the workbooks that I used as punishment.

If a similar thing happened to me these days, I'd laugh with my students at the farting engine and show them how the force created by such a blow-off could be used to run a machine. I would go with their energy and refocus it on learning, without destroying the good feeling created by sharing a joke.

on a wide-hooped skirt and slapping on a disheveled curly red wig and on top of it a large, plumed black hat. Looking like a deranged Little Bopeep, he pranced around the room blowing kisses to his hysterical admirers. The ice was broken. Besides giving the kids a chance to laugh, the teacher had demonstrated, by his willingness to jeopardize his image, that risk has its own rewards and nothing ventured is nothing gained.

Humor, then, is a wonderful way to get kids' attention, to yank them dramatically into a lesson and help them remember the key points of a presentation. It also serves to humanize the learning experience, giving students the opportunity to see adults laugh at themselves, to learn both vicariously and directly to take themselves a little less seriously, thus diminishing some of their fears and insecurities. It's worth repeating that it takes a strong sense of confidence to do this. There is a fine line between being funny and losing the kids' respect. Good teachers find that line and walk it with a firm, steady step, only occasionally slipping on the banana peel.

In doing our background reading for this book, we were struck by the absence of humor in textbooks, in state and national reports, in articles, in research. Education must indeed be a serious enterprise. And yet a lot of funny things happen, or should happen, in classrooms. Only the Teachers of the Year and a few others seemed to think humor merited mentioning. In *Improving Schools from Within,* Roland Barth, himself a former public school teacher and principal, expresses it perfectly: "People learn and grow and survive through humor. We should make an effort to elicit and cultivate it, rather than ignore, thwart, or merely tolerate it."

6

A Funeral for "I Can'ts"

> *"Teachers should not accept failure in*
> *their classroom."*
> —Charles Zezulka
> Connecticut Teacher of the Year

The word "potential" appears frequently in education courses and teaching methods textbooks, which feature grand pronouncements about teachers helping young people grow. Students are tested and evaluated early in their educational careers to measure innate talents that can be developed. Teachers work hard to build on any bit of skill or ability a student may exhibit—one may have a knack for numbers, another may simply get along well with others. Teachers are in the business of spotting and nurturing potential. At least that's what the textbooks and lectures say.

It is interesting that, in all of our discussions with Teachers of the Year, the word "potential" rarely came up. In fact, it was conspicuously absent. Why? Because exceptional teachers make a very clear distinction between hope and conviction. One expresses possibility, the other inevitability. One involves the teacher in an optimistic campaign, the other in a committed crusade. The resolve and toughness that pervade the thinking of great teachers go far beyond hopeful rhetoric. Just listen to the words of Len DeAngelis, Rhode Island's Teacher of the Year: "I find ways, I do what it takes. Sometimes I lose, but I persist. When I lose, I go down fighting."

The same sort of dogged determination is expressed by

Jacquelyn Sweetner Caffey, a Detroit schoolteacher featured in an August 1990 Arts & Entertainment television special, "Who's Minding the Kids? The Truth About Teachers." The relevant segment begins with Caffey stating in no uncertain terms, "I will do anything, as long as it isn't illegal or immoral, to teach my children."

The camera then shifts to a classroom scene in which Caffey is conducting her "Funeral for 'I Can'ts.'" Each student is working on filling out a sheet of paper that says, "I can't _____ as well as my classmates." While the students are filling in the blank and carefully folding the paper once, then twice, Caffey exhorts, "We are going to get rid of these 'I can'ts,' and we don't *ever* want to have them again!"

Beneath a huge banner reading "Funeral for I Can'ts," the children file past a small barbecue, tossing in their "I can'ts" and witnessing the ritualized destruction. This act sends an important message to Caffey's students: "People tell children they can't read. Well, everyone can read. They go by a McDonald's, and they can read that. So you shouldn't tell them they can't read, because they can. I see their reading level not as how empty the glass is but how full, and I keep trying to build it up and up and up."

It would be a mistake to think that all great teachers persist in exactly the same ways. Some are stamped out of the DeAngelis-Caffey mold: tough and strong, they come out swinging. Others persevere with quiet determination. Roberta Ford of Colorado, for example, is a never-say-never type with an emphasis on "caring enough about [students] to see through or see past all the smoke screens they throw in their own way. It takes caring enough to demand the best from them when they're not so sure they even want to try at all. Sometimes, it takes caring when no one else will." Whether it's the symbolism of a "Funeral for I Can'ts" or the "I'll 'care' enough for both of us" message in a poem Ford wrote about one of her students, the bottom line is still the same. Good teachers—excellent teachers—simply don't give up on any of their students.

Caring by Roberta Ford

"I don't care!"

Hostile voice;
Angry child.
We stare at the incomplete assignment.

"I can't do this!"

Your pencil assaults the page.
It gouges out one answer,
Then another.

"Why do I have to have it perfect?"

Your eraser scrubs away thoughtless words.
You answer correctly.

"I really don't care!"

Slowly, almost imperceptibly,
A tear forms and falls,
Then a book slammed shut,
A chair whacked down on the desk top
Signals your exit.

Oh, Michael!
I curse the years of failure and frustration
That made you doubt yourself
And taught you not to try.
I want
To grab you
To hold you
To tell you
That I see through your protests and bravado.

But that's not the way it works with you.

So I calmly call out, "See you tomorrow!"
And turn my head so you don't see me
Watching through the window.

When tomorrow comes,
We'll be at it again, you and I
Gradually you'll yield
To my implacable pursuit.
You'll come to see yourself
As my instincts see you.
My dreams for you will become a reality.

Till then,
I'll "care" enough
For both of us.

"They say that history repeats itself—and, in your case, it might be next semester."

Reprinted by permission of the artist.

Persistence is not only a quality of good teaching: it could well be applied at the core of the American educational system. In the wake of declining test scores and horror stories about illiterates graduating from high school, one knee-jerk solution has been to tighten academic standards. Of course, such methods have no impact on the way teachers teach; it just means that more kids flunk and are held back.

We know that children develop at vastly different rates. It can be a devastating thing for a kid to fail when all he or she needs is a little extra time to grow up and maybe a little extra help along the way. Simply retaining students, making them repeat a grade, turns them into losers. In fact, if ever a practice not only ignored the research but flew in its face, retention is that practice. According to Shepard and Smith in *Flunking Grades: Research and Policies on Retention*:

- Retention in grade has no academic benefit whatsoever. At-risk students who are promoted achieve as well as, or better than, those who are retained.
- Retained students are worse off on all measures of personal and psychological adjustment, self-concept, attitude, and attendance.
- Retained students are 30 percent more likely to drop out than others. Students retained more than once are almost certain to do so.

The evidence indicates that retention and other similar arrangements simply do not work and very likely have long-term effects opposite to those desired. In effect, they create self-fulfilling prophecies.

There is another reason persistence is so important to education and particularly to teaching. Technology has allowed us to communicate and conduct many of our daily transactions with lightning speed. Within hours of the first shots being fired in the Persian Gulf, stock market prices began to drop, not just here but in Japan and Europe as well. Whereas it used to take three days or more for a document to travel coast to coast, there are now overnight express and fax machines. Dinner? No problem. Three minutes in a microwave oven. We tend to forget that some things in life require more time to accomplish and take longer to be felt. Teaching is one such thing. Teachers can never be sure what effect their efforts will have on kids. Their influence is subtle and far-reaching.

James Ellingson, Minnesota's Teacher of the Year, often teaches

*It can be a devastating thing
for a kid to fail when all
he or she needs is a little extra
time to grow up.*

39

in themes to integrate his curriculum. One of his themes is "winter," a particularly important topic in his state. He takes his classes of fourth and fifth graders for a whole day of cross-country skiing, during which they must dress for the cold, cook for themselves, and account for every wrapper and piece of plastic. These activities lead naturally into lessons—on hypothermia, nutrition, the environment.

Two years ago, Ellingson received a call from Joe, a former student who was now married and the father of two children. "I hear you like to go fishing, walleye fishing. I'd like to take you fishing." So they went fishing, and halfway out to the lake Ellingson asked him, "What made you think of me? I haven't seen you in a long time."

Joe replied, "Well, I've been thinking about myself and my life. You taught me something a long time ago that I'll never forget."

"Really, what's that?" Ellingson asked.

"Well, you know the day you took us to the winter woods? I was the group leader of four other kids. And you told me that we were to take off the wrappers of all the materials we had and leave them at school and repackage everything into four or five plastic baggies. And we had to prove to you when we returned that we still had the baggies. I still remember our motto: 'Take only memories, leave only footprints.'" Ellingson hadn't remembered this, but Joe obviously had. His final comment was "I'm going to teach my kids the same way."

As Henry Adams, the nineteenth-century writer-philosopher, once commented, "A teacher affects eternity. He can never tell where his influence stops." Truly exceptional teachers seem to know this instinctively. They are not overly concerned with little twists and turns in the road. A breakdown is not a catastrophe; a detour does not end the trip. Like Len DeAngelis and James Ellingson, these teachers can see beyond the bend, over the hill, all the way to the horizon. With such a long journey stretching out in front of them, they see little relevance to the words "I can't."

"Potential" doesn't make it either. It smacks of uncertainty and doubt.

The special teachers we have come to know are pluggers. They have grit and guts. They have the spunk of a bulldog, the stamina of a marathon runner. In their classrooms, perseverance is the principle.

7

More Rainbows Than Rain

"The single most accurate predictor of
success is self-esteem."
—**Bill Nave**
Maine Teacher of the Year

Rod Laird's principal approached him with a request: Would he take Max in his core class? It seemed Max had drawn a knife on his core teacher, and unless Rod would agree to give him one last chance he was to be expelled.

Whoa! Just a minute here. Pulled a knife?! This is not talking back or being rowdy. This goes beyond the standard "attitude problem." But, against his own better judgment, Rod, Wyoming's Teacher of the Year, agreed to give it a try.

It turned out Max was no "tough guy" at all. In fact, he was courteous, kind, and hard-working He lived in a dirt-floored adobe house with his brothers and sisters and a mother who did her best to provide a home on almost no income. Despite these material difficulties, in class Max was reliable, respectful, conscientious. He gave the assignments his best shot, usually earning a C.

On Saturdays Max would sometimes visit Rod at home. On one of these visits Rod discovered that Max dearly wanted to go "plinking"—shooting at tin cans or pine cones—in the hills with his friends but, of course, had no rifle. Rod loaned him his old Winchester 90, a family heirloom. Each Saturday evening it would come back cleaned and oiled, with never a scratch.

Much later in the year, Rod finally asked Max the puzzling

Increasingly, teachers are the only positive influence in many kids' lives.

question: "How in the world did you ever come to pull a knife on your teacher?" A look of sadness fell over Max's face as he related how she had ridiculed and humiliated him, until one day he could stand it no more, and something had snapped. It is a classic tale of how one person tore someone down, while another built him up.

Self-esteem is the assessment we make of our own worth. Kids with low self-esteem feel powerless. They blame others for their failures, avoid difficult situations, and are poor students regardless of their natural abilities. They are vulnerable to pressures from their peers and the media, easily manipulated, easily frustrated. When pushed hard, they can become a knife-wielding Max.

Children with high self-esteem, in contrast, are capable of making sound decisions, are proud of their accomplishments, are willing to take responsibility, and are able to cope with frustration. They learn to view their failures and mistakes as positive learning experiences. They are free to be creative, because they are willing to meet challenges and take risks in new situations. They have the power to accomplish their plans, influence their environments, and become the best students they can.

Teachers have always played a critical role in determining which path a young person will follow. In the preface to *Teacher and Child*, Hiam Ginott makes this poignant appraisal of a teacher's power:

> I have come to a frightening conclusion. I am the decisive element in the classroom. It is my daily mood that makes the weather. As a teacher, I possess tremendous power to make a child's life miserable or joyous. I can be a tool of torture or an instrument of inspiration. I can humiliate or humor, hurt or heal. In all situations, it is my response that decides whether a crisis will be escalated or deescalated and a child humanized or dehumanized.

The teacher stands at the crossroads day in and day out, sending signals and messages. Each message is either hurtful or healing, uplifting or downgrading. Every interaction is saying, "this way or that."

And if this characterization was true in the past, it is even more so today. Whereas it used to be the school's job to see to a child's academic development, and home and church took care of the behavioral and moral components, increasingly, teachers are the only positive influence in many kids lives and school the only stable environment. The divorce rate has doubled since 1950. Nearly 25 percent of children under 18 are living in a single-parent home. Only 7 percent of school-age children live in a two-parent home with a single wage earner. More preschool children are in day care than are at home. Nearly 2 million children live with neither parent. Kids and their parents spend more time watching TV than talking. By default, the primary responsibility for imparting the values traditionally taught and nurtured at home has landed at the classroom doorstep.

What can teachers do to help children build self-esteem? We think the answer has two parts, and Bill Nave, cofounder of a highly successful alternative school for dropouts in Turner, Maine, gives us a good start: "The cornerstone of good teaching, as of any human relationship, is a belief in the intrinsic worth of each student. This belief leads directly to an absolute respect and acceptance of each student as the person he or she is."

Research indicates that most children enter school bright-eyed, enthusiastic, and eager to learn. By the fourth grade, however, there has been a dramatic decline in the way they view themselves.

> *"The cornerstone of good teaching is a belief in the intrinsic worth of each student."*

Schools do not deliberately foster this decline, nor is it necessarily inevitable. What happens is that by fourth grade children have run head on into the social and educational realities of peer pressure, competition, and failure. Many find out very early that they are not as smart as other kids or as popular or as athletic or as creative or as well-dressed or as affluent. While this may make no difference to a 3- or 4-year-old, it becomes increasingly important to the emotional well-being of an 8- or 9-year-old and even more so to that of a 13- or 14-year-old.

None of this is new. What *is* new is that, as a corollary of the changes in the family described earlier, children are not getting the home support that is vital to establishing and sustaining a strong, healthy self-image. When they get home, there often is no one there to encourage them and help put their daily problems and frustrations into perspective. At the age of 13 or 14 (or 8 or 9), they are left to fend for themselves, to judge what's really important and what isn't, to analyze realistically their personal strengths and weaknesses, to come to grips with the burdens of peer pressure and the constant bombardment of media-generated role models.

Nina Fue, New Jersey Teacher of the Year, has taught on the elementary level for over thirty years. She sees the changes in the family structure as one of the most critical issues in education today. However, rather than throw her hands up and shout in the wind, she takes the problem on, secure in the conviction that she can deal with the world as it is and still make a difference. "As teachers we can't look at the world the way we think it ought to be, but we have to deal with it the way it is. . . . Sometimes coming to school is the only stable thing that happens in some children's lives. They come to school concerned about problems at home with parents or with peers. Sometimes the only safe place where they know they have rules to follow and certain obligations to meet is the classroom."

Dr. Betsey Geddes, an inner-city school principal quoted in *High Risk,* echoes Fue's commitment. "As educators, we can't all say parents must do their work at home or we won't do our jobs at school. In some cases parents won't or can't. It may be frightening that many of our kids are raised on school food, don't know how to use a knife and fork properly, or don't know what is acceptable social behavior. . . . But if that's what a child needs to learn," she continues, "then that is where we need to start. It is a great opportunity to help change things and there is no one else to do it."

Now we come to the second part of the answer to our question. We know the importance of self-esteem in the developmental process, and showing a willingness to accept responsibility for building students' self-esteem is a necessary component of effective teaching. But to get young people "feeling good" about themselves should not be an end in itself. It is only the means to an end. "Feeling good" is just the first step to 'doing good." It does not get

══════ Doing Bad and ══════ Feeling Good

A standardized math test was given to 13-year-olds in six countries last year. Koreans did the best. Americans did the worst, coming in behind Spain, Britain, Ireland and Canada. Now the bad news. Besides being shown triangles and equations, the kids were shown the statement "I am good at mathematics." Koreans came last in this category. Only 23% answered yes. Americans were No. 1, with an impressive 68% in agreement.

American students may not know their math, but they have evidently absorbed the lessons of the newly fashionable self-esteem curriculum wherein kids are taught to feel good about themselves. Of course, it is not just educators who are convinced that feeling good is the key to success. The Governor of Maryland recently announced the formation of a task force on self-esteem, "a 23-member panel created on the theory," explains the *Baltimore Sun*, "that drug abuse, teen pregnancy, failure in school and most social ills can be reduced by making people feel good about themselves." Judging by the international math test, such task forces may be superfluous. Kids already feel exceedingly good about doing bad.

Source: Charles Krauthammer, *Time*, February 5, 1990, p. 78.

47

the job done. Teachers must do more than show their students that they care. They must engage in ego-boosting behaviors every day so that practical successes can be realized.

After our discussions with teachers and a review of current research, we can offer a short list of approaches that successful teachers use to help kids feel good *and* do well.

- They help children recognize and focus personal strengths. Everyone has talents and abilities, although these will differ from person to person. A poor speller may be a very good artist. A poor artist may have a fine singing voice.
- They listen, without prejudgment, to what students have to say. They take them seriously. This tells kids that their thoughts and ideas are important.
- They have high but reasonable expectations for children. Building self-esteem does not mean having kids feel good about doing poorly. It means having them feel good about doing the best they can.
- They build a sense of responsibility in students. This provides an important base for the development of self-esteem. Students who are given appropriate responsibilities learn that their actions can contribute directly to what happens in their lives.
- They use "I" statements when correcting students. "I feel angry" is a better response to give a child than "You make me mad." "I need your work so that I will have something to base your grade on" is a better approach than "You are lazy and irresponsible."
- They act as a model of acceptable behavior. They do as they say, demonstrating positive and responsible behaviors for children to learn from. They know they can't expect kids to treat each other with respect if they don't show consideration for all children in the class.

- They praise children when they do well or make a worthy effort. This helps build confidence and a positive self-image, better enabling children to face challenges.
- They help kids understand that feelings are important and that there are appropriate ways of expressing them.
- They use mistakes as an opportunity to teach rather than to embarrass or ridicule. To overcome the paralyzing effects of failure that afflict so many children and so dramatically interfere with their ability to learn or try, good teachers stress the positive aspects of mistakes and help children recognize that failure on an assignment doesn't make them a failure in life.

Good teachers understand the value of building a child's self-esteem, as well as the importance of treating all students as valuable, contributing members of the classroom. In the words of Gloria Anderson, Teacher of the Year from Virginia, teachers who take this positive approach create "more rainbows than rain" for their students.

"But isn't it more important to learn how to be a decent human being?"

Reprinted by permission of the artist.

8

Dinner at Abigail's

"Teachers must learn from other teachers."
—Mary Kay Baker
Indiana Teacher of the Year

In a recent Gallup poll conducted in conjunction with the National Education Association, 231 semifinalists in the "Thanks to Teachers" competition were asked to pinpoint key tools that helped them do their jobs. A whopping 84 percent listed "meeting with teachers and other colleagues" as helping them "a great deal," more than release time, having their own office or phone, or having more support staff to help with clerical duties.

Why would such a high percentage of exemplary teachers place such importance on teacher talk? They are already good. What else do they need to know? Well, one of the things they know is that successful teaching is a dynamic process—what worked terrifically with last year's class may bomb this year. They also know that the highly regimented nature of the teacher's working life can, over time, sap them of their professional vitality and creativity. And because they are in the business of learning, they need to be alert for things that will enhance the quality of their output and their ability to stay current and fresh. So there is always room for improvement, a new angle, a different approach.

But, in the real world, teaching is isolating work, and teachers do not have very much to do with each other. They are secluded in what one teacher we know has called their "adjoining caves." Information on policies and procedures flows down in memos from

Collaboration between teachers is the exception, not the rule.

administrators, and teachers spend their days in the classroom implementing these policies.

Consequently, teachers don't feel that they have ownership of the process. Sequestered in their adjoining caves, they have little opportunity to discuss their profession. There is minimal sharing of ideas and techniques. Collaboration between and among teachers is the exception, not the rule. Teachers are divided and, to some extent, conquered—dispirited and disengaged.

The culture of teaching is conducive to solitude. Teachers' competence is seen as coming from formal education—they are required to take certain courses before becoming certified and must sometimes accumulate additional course work within a specified period of time. Then they are periodically "in-serviced," the teaching equivalent of having the oil changed in the car (whether it needs it or not). These in-service programs tend to be imposed by school boards, superintendents, and principals, whose views on what teachers need to know do not necessarily coincide with those of the teachers themselves. There is often no sustained follow-up—teachers are expected to implement the ideas presented in these sessions without any opportunity for the discussion of problems as they arise. Questions go unanswered, frustrations develop, and the teachers return to their caves to wait to be "in-serviced" on the next topic.

Teachers do not agree with this emphasis. The National Center for Education Information's *Profile of Teachers in the U.S.—1990* asked participants which of eight items had contributed most to their development of competence as a teacher in each of seven areas. In most of the areas represented, "my own teaching experiences" was chosen as the most important factor. And despite the fact that "education courses" and "in-service activities" were among the choices, "other teachers" was generally perceived to be the second most important factor in developing competence.

Finding time to talk is a problem, however. After preparing for classes, teaching them, correcting work, holding conferences with parents and students, completing the necessary paperwork, and carrying out other duties, there is little or no time left for discussing teaching with colleagues. Many teachers simply don't see their colleagues during the course of the day, and, if they do, it's usually during the half-hour lunch break.

This "cocooning" is perhaps hardest on new teachers, who desperately need input and feedback. In many school districts, fledgling teachers commonly get the toughest classes and the most duties and are then asked to coach cheerleading, be the student government adviser, contribute a few articles to the school paper, help out at the Thursday night choral concert, be the teacher representative at the monthly PTA meeting, bake some cookies for the latest fund-raiser. . . . This "boot camp" atmosphere, often fostered unintentionally by the schools, is a major contributor to the enormously high turnover rate of new teachers, who feel both overwhelmed and isolated.

The best teachers manage to break down the barriers between adjoining caves, regardless of the obstacles. They know the dangers of what Pamela Johnson, Iowa's Teacher of the Year, calls the "self-contaminated classroom," and they work hard to avoid the numbness that results. From our research and our discussion with teachers, this barrier-busting appears to take two forms: *taking* and *giving*.

First, *taking*—good teaching techniques and excellent lessons come from a process of trial and error, in which ideas, methods, and procedures are adapted to the needs of both students and teacher. No individual, no textbook, no curriculum guide, no workshop can be the repository of all the successful, or potentially successful, things that go on daily in thousands of classrooms across the country.

"*I*'m not certain anything I do is totally original."

Len DeAngelis of Rhode Island unashamedly admits to stealing potentially interesting lessons, peering into other teachers' classrooms while on his duty period. Texas Teacher of the Year Mercedes Bonner stresses the value of "lounge ideas," advice and assistance gathered informally in the teachers' room. Carolyn Baldwin, Teacher of the Year from Montana, sums up the feeling of many outstanding teachers: "Go in the rooms and watch. See how successful teachers communicate and interact and make a difference in their children's lives. And take from those teachers the qualities, the methods, the techniques that will work best for you, so that you have this little cache of styles and ideas that you're taking along with you."

A teacher's peers are a potential source of ideas to be tested in the classroom and reshaped, adapted, expanded, modified like crazy. Teachers' ideas about teaching are community property. Barbara Firestone, Kansas Teacher of the Year, makes this clear when she says, "The teachers with whom I've worked over the years have done and are doing wonderful things with children. Because of their influence, I'm not certain anything I do is totally original."

As to *giving*, the good ideas a teacher develops or is exposed to need to be shared with others: the other side of "creative swiping" is "relentless sharing." For this to work, school districts need to schedule common planning times for teachers to meet and discuss general concerns and search for solutions to problems. It means fashioning an environment in which teachers' ideas are looked upon as signs of vitality, not nuisances. It means in-service programs that are planned jointly by administrators *and* teachers. It means budgeting and providing time for in- and out-of-district workshops and conferences. It means devising programs like West

Virginia's Teachers' Academy, in which successful practitioners meet, share ideas and strategies, and return to their counties and regions to pass on what they've learned.

There is a sense of professional obligation that really great teachers seem to have in common. They don't, according to Marilyn Grondel of Utah, "keep ideas and materials secret. A successful teacher becomes even more successful by 'dialoguing' with colleagues and sharing ideas and materials."

And then there is dinner at Abigail's. In a January 1989 article in *NEA Today*, Madeleine Grumet talks about her work with the faculty of Mynderse Academy in Seneca Falls, New York. The academy is one of twenty-six public schools in the nation selected to participate in NEA's Mastery in Learning Project (MIL). Designed to encourage and support teacher development, teacher empowerment, and curriculum change, MIL requires that teachers get together to determine what they need to do to improve the learning environment, working relationships, and curriculum of their schools.

The emphasis of Grumet's article is not so much on specifics of

Reprinted by permission of the artist.

Teachers who are given the time and place to communicate with each other as a group can produce inspiring results.

the program as on the value of "nurturing collaboration." "At first, we in the Mynderse project met in the library after school," she states. "Representatives to the project steering committee came when they could. But it was difficult."

Difficult? Why? Because of the problems we have already discussed: the atmosphere for collaboration didn't exist, nor did teachers have the time. "The teachers were tired, had to leave for other meetings, were reluctant to give up time set aside to help students with class assignments. We persevered, trying to shape the project with whomever was there—but our project didn't start to come together until the night we had dinner at Abigail's."

Abigail's represents a complete contrast to the isolation and intellectual loneliness of the classrooms and corridors of the school. You see, Abigail's is a local restaurant where diners sit at big tables, family-style, as relish trays, soups, salads, and desserts appear in regular sequence. The rolls pass down the table as serving trays fly left and right and butter and sour cream zig-zag their way back and forth. As you'd expect in such a place, the conversation is animated and unstructured—no agenda, no formality.

For the members of the Mynderse MIL project, Abigail's was not a new experience. Over the years they had come there with their families to celebrate birthdays, graduations, anniversaries, and even an occasional Thanksgiving when someone didn't want to cook. As Grumet describes it, "Abigail's served murmurs and memories of warmth and intimacy."

"Cocooning" is not possible there. The concept of "adjoining caves" wouldn't make it past the front door of Abigail's. And that's the idea! Teachers who are given the time and place to communicate with each other as a group can produce inspiring results.

In fact, we suggest that teachers heed the appeal at the end of Grumet's article: "Join them at Abigail's sometime. You will see that in an environment that invites exchange, collegiality, and self-esteem, teachers are confident, generous and creative. Provided with conditions that permit them to work together to address the real issues that face them and their students, teachers can and do change schools."

9

Little Sharks

*"The students know the rules and the
consequences of breaking them."*
—Debbie Pace Silver
Louisiana Teacher of the Year

Muttered by red-eyed young teachers, the words "I just want to teach" usually express the exasperation of having to deal with the inordinate load of paperwork just dumped on them (due yesterday, in triplicate) or with a student or an entire classroom run amok.

The 1990 NBC White Paper titled "To Be a Teacher," presented by Tom Brokaw, captures this frustration well. As the camera pans over the class of first-year mathematics teacher Andrea Geddick, Brokaw talks about the need to motivate and discipline students who simply don't care. Two girls are giggling, another student is yawning, and another has his head on the desk. "At one point I was writing on the board, and I felt the tears were right there," Geddick says. "I was all ready to just let go. . . . But, no, I was strong," she continues. "I usually save my serious crying for the ride home."

In another scene, the camera shows two girls sharing answers. Geddick confronts them as the rest of the class looks on. "I'll be forced to take action. I will. . . . I have before. You can ask people. . . . You think it's funny?"

This scenario is played out every day in a thousand different variations in classrooms across the country. It may be a minor skirmish lasting only a few seconds, or it may be a full-fledged

"*I*'d rather die and go to hell than be a first-year teacher again. "

battle. The one thing most disruptions have in common is that new teachers are inadequately prepared to deal with them.

When the National Center for Education Information was preparing its *Profile of Teachers in the U.S.—1990,* it asked the question "When you first started teaching, how well did your teaching preparation program prepare you for the classroom management/discipline aspects of teaching?" A majority of respondents (53 percent) said either "not well" or "not well at all."

Ben Jimenez, who, along with Jaime Escalante of *Stand and Deliver* fame, has had spectacular success teaching advanced math to the mostly underprivileged Latino students of Garfield High School in East Los Angeles, says that his college studies did little to prepare him for the realities of inner-city teaching. The *Los Angeles Times Magazine* quotes him as saying, "What chance do you have to deal with the theories of Piaget and Montessori when you've got a kid who is kicking a trash can across the room?" After his first year of teaching, he had doubts about returning: "I thought it wasn't for me. You want to save the world. You want to help. But the kids are a bunch of little sharks. They'll take advantage of you if they can."

Most teachers vividly remember the numbing helplessness they felt when confronted with their first case of open defiance, their first class out of control—noise level approaching that of an airliner on takeoff and bodies careening off desks and walls. Paper airplanes, spitballs, rubber bands fill the classroom air. You *care* about these kids, you have something to teach them, you've spent hours preparing lesson plans, and they're going bonkers. No wonder more than one experienced teacher has said, "I'd rather die and go to hell than be a first-year teacher again." Certainly nothing can destroy a new teacher's enthusiasm faster and smash his or her idealism and sense of commitment quicker than discipline problems.

Yet most veteran teachers find discipline problems only a "minor barrier" to effective teaching. At the bottom of this page are the responses to one of the questions posed to the 231 semifinalists in the "Thanks to Teachers" competition. Discipline problems come in a dead last as a major barrier, following such things as

The Main Obstacles to Effective Teaching

There are a number of different things that get in the way of effective teaching. How much of a barrier to your ability to teach at full capacity is each of the following—a major barrier, a minor one, or no barrier at all?

	Major Barrier	Minor Barrier	Not a Barrier
a. Insufficient funds for supplies and materials	40%	38%	22%
b. Not having enough time to prepare for classes	39	43	18
c. Too many children in classes	33	38	29
d. Administrative bureaucracy	29	46	25
e. Lack of technology equipment	28	44	28
f. Lack of parental involvement	25	48	27
g. Lack of technology training	22	49	29
h. Non-teaching duties: lunchroom duty, study halls, etc.	20	39	41
i. Not being allowed to design own courses	11	38	51
j. Discipline problems in your classroom	10	54	36

Source: NEA Today, December 1990, p. 24. Reprinted by permission.

"*You'll find* Classroom Discipline in Three Easy Lessons *in fiction.*"

Reprinted by permission of the artist.

"lack of parental involvement" and "too many children in classes." Even "administrative bureaucracy" poses a larger problem for teachers than discipline.

After the remarks of Andrea Geddick and Ben Jimenez, how can this be? Well, as with many of the skills necessary for good teaching, the successful confrontation of discipline problems comes from experience, from having to deal directly with the situation and learning from it. Practice teaching provides some sense of direction, but being alone in someone else's classroom is not the same as maintaining control in your own. After all, a cooperating teacher is not lurking in the hall to step in and read the class the riot act.

Prevention—anticipating and dealing with disruptions *before* they occur—is the key to limiting discipline problems. Admittedly, it's tough for new teachers to apply this principle, because they are often unaware of the signs until the paper planes are flying in full formation. Employing a technique used by Debbie Pace Silver and other effective teachers, Ben Jimenez returned his second year with a list of rules that he stuck to from the first day. He clearly communicated at the start of the year the behavior he expected from students and delineated the consequences of any breaches in that code. He also borrowed a technique from his old high school mathematics teacher. Each day starts with a quiz. It helps settle the class and sets the tone for what follows.

Other techniques employed by experienced teachers include being aware of what's going on in the classroom at all times and moving around a lot, scanning the room for signs of possible problems and dealing with them before they develop. Effective teachers keep the lesson moving, keep students alert and on task by asking questions, and are aware of which students are likely to precipitate trouble.

In our discussions with Teachers of the Year, we also picked up a few more hints. Anne Neidhardt, Teacher of the Year from Maryland, stresses the importance of being confident. "When you walk into a classroom," she says, "your sense of yourself at that time translates so quickly to the students. . . .We need to keep ourselves calm and positive and feeling in control, and that gives the students a lot of security. Then they feel calm and in control of that lesson, too. And things are going to go so much better for everyone." She also notes the importance of being organized, with the lesson thoughtfully planned and all equipment, materials for demonstration, and handouts ready. "All of this should be right at your fingertips, and you should feel comfortable with it."

Others stress the importance of fairness. Kids have a hyperdeveloped sense of right and wrong, especially where actions toward themselves are concerned. Most know when they've messed up and will accept the consequences as long as they are fair and fit the circumstances. One caution, though. Some adolescents seem to spend all their time pointing out the unfairness of things. "That's not fair" is their response to everything that goes against their preconceived notions of the universe. But teachers should stick to their guns.

Part of being fair is being consistent about what is considered unacceptable behavior. However, it is still important to respect

"Seldom is progress made by protecting students from the consequences of their behavior."

individual differences when disciplining students who cross the line. Sometimes a look is enough. With others a talk will do. Some seem to respond only to firm reprimands or after-school detention.

Among other good advice we heard, teachers should avoid forcing a child into a position where he or she has to defy them to save face. Arguing will just cause the situation to escalate. Differences should be settled out in the hall or after school when tempers have had a chance to cool.

A teacher should never threaten something unless prepared to follow it through. Ineffectual parents make a habit of threatening all sorts of dumb and devastating consequences for bad behavior or poor grades—"You are never going to be allowed to leave this house again." Teachers may very well be the first people in children's lives who say what they mean and mean what they say. Teacher Duane Obermier of Nebraska says, "Seldom is progress made by protecting students from the consequences of their behavior."

Yelling is fruitless. It hurts the throat, and the kids soon get used to it and pay no attention or, worse yet, egg teachers on until they're walking Sucrets commercials. Smashing a meterstick on a desk, whistling loudly, or scratching the fingernails down the blackboard will get their attention in a dramatic way.

There is no use in holding grudges. This is a tough one, but as Anne Neidhardt says, "regardless of how they may behave one day, that's one day. The next day we go in and it's a new day, and we need to give the students a new opportunity regardless of who has given us a hard time. We need to give them the opportunity to do the right thing and be good students the following day." The teacher must strive to be objective, focusing not on the person but on the behavior. It is essential to make it clear that the difficulty is with the actions, not with the person doing them.

It is the teacher's classroom and the teacher who is in charge. It is not wise to rely too heavily on the threat of "the office." This just diminishes the teacher's authority and bothers the administrator.

And finally, after a long string of don'ts, here's a big, universal do. Len DeAngelis of Rhode Island has taught in a variety of places, including the inner city. He believes that the key to maintaining classroom discipline is in presenting exciting lessons. "If you make your lesson interesting enough," he says, "then the kids will respond. They can't help it."

The bottom line is this: Discipline problems don't exist in America's best classrooms. The recipe Teachers of the Year and others use to create the proper learning environment involves an ounce of prevention, a cup of organization, one tablespoon each of fairness and follow-through, and a pinch of excitement. It also takes time to figure all this out—it isn't obvious, and it doesn't happen overnight.

New teachers have no history with the kids and few experiences to help guide their thinking and actions. But their "rep" will soon develop if they work hard, learn from those early problems, and stick around awhile. And there is also the consolation that at least one person we know of can sympathize. . . .

"Come on, Jimmy, time to get up. It's the first day of school."

"Aw, ma, I don't want to go."

"Come on now, your oatmeal's getting cold."

> **"*If you make your lesson interesting enough, the kids will respond. They can't help it.*"**

"Ma, I don't want to go. The kids don't like me. They call me names and write bad stuff about me on the bathroom walls."

"That only happened a few times last year, son. I'm sure things will be better this year. Now, come on. It's getting late."

"I don't want to go. The teachers pick on me. They're all out to get me. Please let me stay home. I'll clean the house."

"Jimmy, I don't need any help. What I need is for you to get up and get to school. Now I'm going to count to three. One . . . "

"Ma, I think I'm going to be sick."

"That's it, Jimmy! I'm tired of going through this every year. Now, GET UP! You've got to go to school. After all, you *are* the principal."

10

Hunting for Worms

*"Schooling should not be viewed as a
spectator sport for students, where adults
perform while students watch."*

—**Pamela Adams Johnson**
Iowa Teacher of the Year

How do we make learning relevant and meaningful to kids? Well, let's start with an example. James Ellingson is standing on the lawn next to his school in Moorehead, Minnesota, on a lovely spring day. A 60' x 100' rectangle of grass has been marked off. He is talking about "protective coloration" with his fourth-grade class.

"Imagine today that robins are taking advantage of the spring weather to go hunting for worms and that we are the worms," he says. "What color worm do you want to be?"

He begins to sprinkle "worms"—300 colored toothpicks—onto the rectangle. There are red ones, blue ones, green, yellow, and natural. Sixty of each. Like all good scientists, the students make predictions.

"I don't want to be red, that's for sure."

"If I was green, they'd never find me."

Eighteen kids then collect data. They get down on their hands and knees and try to find as many toothpicks as they can. All the reds are counted. Then the blues. Only 7 of 60 green toothpicks are found, which represents a fraction. There is a brief discussion of fractions. To compare fractions, the students draw five columns to represent the numbers of each color found. The numbers range from a low of 7 to a high of 56—yellow worms are a robin's feast. The class has produced a graph.

How do we make learning relevant and meaningful to kids? By making it jump off the page of the textbook. By breathing life into it. By making it irresistibly interesting.

Unfortunately, most teachers don't practice a "hunting for worms" method of teaching. They opt instead to produce and deliver lectures composed of facts, facts, and more facts. Students are expected to sit quietly and absorb what is spoken *at* them. Eyes front. No moving around and no doodling. The teacher plans, presents, and keeps order. It's all very neat and exact, with the teacher's responsibility ending once students have been told what they are required to remember.

It's tradition. We teach the way we were taught, the practice being handed down like a family heirloom. Indeed, as is noted in the 1990 *Nation's Report Card* published by the National Assessment of Educational Progress, "across the past 20 years, little seems to

"Mr. Stein makes us memorize stuff. We call him 'King of the Rote.'"

Reprinted by permission of the artist.

*O*ur schools, with their reliance on routine, order, and repetition, are a natural haven for boredom.

have changed in how students are taught. Despite much research suggesting alternatives, classrooms still appear to be dominated by textbooks, teacher lectures, and short-answer activity sheets."

In *The Republic,* Plato states that educators should remember their aim is not to "put into the mind knowledge that was not there before," though they may do that within limits, but "to turn the mind's eye to the light so that it can see for itself." An old Chinese proverb hints at the same thing: "I hear and I forget; I see and I remember; I do and I understand." A teacher's business is not to stick thoughts into children's heads but to make them think for themselves.

If lecturing *at* people didn't work in Greece in 400 B.C. or in ancient China, why should we believe it will work today? Our kids are brought up on Nintendo and MTV. They are used to being entertained by Madison Avenue. This is the Teflon generation—little, certainly not a long-winded lecture, seems to stick to these kids. Our nation's classrooms are not populated by dummies; the students are just brain-numbingly bored. And our schools, with their reliance on routine, order, and repetition, are a natural haven for boredom.

The critical question, then, is not "What does a *teacher* do?" That's not the focus we want or the perspective that good teachers adopt. It should be "What does a teacher get the *kids* to do?" Learning should be an active, participatory affair. It's not enough just to tell children things. They need to know how to interpret what they hear and how to relate it to what else they know. They need to touch, taste, and feel the subject. They require stimulation and excitation. Whenever possible, students need to experience what is being taught.

To bring learning alive and make it meaningful to students, teachers have to be both creative and inspired. For example, a November 17, 1990, article in the *Los Angeles Times* reported that kindergarten teacher Arlene Johnston had won the first national Excellence in Geography Teaching Award for her method of teaching 5-year-olds the locations of the fifty states. Her kindergartners defeated a group of high school students in a competition to locate states on a blank map and then identify their best-known products and nicknames.

How did Johnston's geniuses do it? According to the article, "Johnston accomplished the task without high-priced programs or a battery of research. She just asked the children to send letters to friends and relatives in all 50 states and posted them on a map in the classroom until every state was represented." Her school received a collection of geography materials, Johnston won $10,000, "and it [was] proved, once again, that an imaginative teacher and a captivated class of students are still the best combination for successful education on critical concepts."

Another example? In a recent A&E education special titled "Who's Minding the Kids? The Truth About Teachers," Karen Cahill, a fourth- and fifth-grade teacher in Boston, is seen doing math problems at the blackboard. The number on the board is the cost of a pair of Adidas sneakers. And the question is "If you buy two pairs of Adidas sneakers, how much is it going to cost you?" She tells the show's host, "They don't want to know what it means if Dick has 25 apples in his cart and Jane has 15. They don't care about Dick and Jane. They want Adidas." In writing class, she has them draft letters to people who have hurt them. It's a therapeutic exercise that illustrates, in a very personal way, how good communication skills are useful in dealing with the problems in kids' lives.

We tend to divide our school days into little compartments—35 minutes for science, 25 for social studies—but good teachers are constantly looking for ways to create linkages between subjects. Howard Selekman, Teacher of the Year from Pennsylvania, suggested to us that "decompartmentalizing our curriculum" is critical to the success of teachers and schools. "Number one is to develop a strongly interdisciplinary atmosphere in our schools." "Hunting for worms" is a good example of math and science being taught at the same time. Or the day's vocabulary and spelling lessons can reinforce words learned earlier in the day during a science or history lesson.

Overcoming boredom and indifference can also be accomplished by encouraging active participation in school lessons. In the example below, the difference between *studying* and *doing*

= Scratch-and-Sniff Science =

Textbooks have been banned in the elementary science curriculum in Mesa, Arizona; instead, teachers use kits. The kits are simple materials given to each small group of students so that they can, after a short presentation by the teacher, do an "experiment" themselves. "Clay boats," for example, is a problem solving, generalization, and creativity exercise for third graders at Hermosa Vista Elementary. After a brief demonstration by the teacher of objects that float and objects that sink, students list properties of buoyant objects, such as size, shape, and composition. Then, students get water-filled plastic containers plus a lump of clay to shape into something that floats. There are squeals of delight at success, groans when the clay sinks.

At North High School in Downers Grove, Illinois, first-year chemistry students are locked in battle over the shape of C_2H_5OH molecules. Several have climbed atop their desks as they attempt to create the molecular structure of grain alcohol. "I can't teach kids 'til I've hooked them," Bob Lewis, their teacher, says. "This is five shows a day." Lewis's first law of dynamic teaching is simple: the more involved students get pursuing science, the longer they will retain their lessons. One of Lewis's students, Lisa Chen, a junior studying advanced chemistry, is living proof: "The classes are fast. You wish you could understand more, and eventually you do."

Source: Newsweek, April 9, 1990, p. 61, and *Newsweek Special Education,* Fall-Winter 1990, p. 24.

science is illustrated. Call it "hands on" learning, call it "involvement based" pedagogy, the fact is that games, experiments, puzzles, computer simulations, field studies, group projects, and role playing are all ways to get in there and get dirty.

While the sciences are a natural area for "scratch and sniff" learning, it can be done and is being done with all subjects. Terry Weeks, Tennessee's 1988 Teacher of the Year, teaches history by having students act the parts of citizens at a town meeting debating a historical issue or as legislators researching, writing, introducing, and debating bills. "These strategies allow the students to think for themselves," Weeks notes, "and they reaffirm the importance of the individual in making history."

The picture that we have painted here is of a different kind of classroom. It is one in which the teacher takes on the role of provocateur, devil's advocate, conductor, facilitator, and guide. Ted Sizer, a Brown University professor and a leading innovator in education, often speaks of his "fantasy school" where, among other things, students are active learners—"student as worker," as Sizer calls it—and teachers are coaches, not lecturers who merely deliver information. In such a fantasy school, clay boats, kindergarten geography, and worm-hunting would be the rule, not the exception.

11

Of Madrigals and Milites Romani

*"Energy, enthusiasm, excitement are what
spark a good teacher."*
—Len DeAngelis
Rhode Island Teacher of the Year

The world of a baby begins to change at about 6 months of age. Prior to that, the little person is largely confined to a crib or stroller with nothing much to see or do. After that, muscles strengthen and bones harden. Yippee! The Age of Mobility. Crawling opens new horizons, and exploration is the name of the game. Pretty soon mom and dad are back at the store buying items to "babyproof" the house—plugs for the electrical outlets, gates for the staircases, and locks for the cabinets.

The newly mobile baby shows the desire to learn that is characteristic of the human species. Curiosity reigns supreme among the crawling set. Behind every door is something delightful and magical. Around every corner is a wonderful new experience to be picked up and tasted. Any item within reach is pushed and pulled to find out what it does.

At about 2 years of age, language becomes another means of inquiry, and, for the next several years, the youngster is the perfect journalist. Every sentence begins with an interrogative pronoun. Who is that, mommy? What makes it do that? When will we be there? Where are we going? Why, daddy, why?

"*W*e take natural curiosity and self-motivation and peel it away. "

And then comes school. In the process of fitting them into the institution and quantifying the degree to which they succeed, we begin to rob young people of the natural joy of learning. The hunger to learn, a spontaneous aspect of early childhood, is transformed on the battleground of homework and report cards. Raymond Wlodkowski and Judith Jaynes describe this metamorphosis in an intriguing book, *Eager to Learn*. In the opening chapter, they describe three "potential diminishers of motivation to learn."

First, there is the design of the graded school. It does not take school-age youngsters long to realize that school is very different from home. School has rules for everything, including where you can sit, when you can speak, and when you can go to the bathroom. The day is chopped into numerous discrete units for learning that are ushered in and out by ringing bells. Chaz Zezulka, Connecticut's Teacher of the Year, talked about this pigeonholing, conventionalizing system with us: "We take natural curiosity and self-motivation and peel it away. We box learning. We grade it. We degrade it. We label. We track. We categorize so that learning is almost no longer recognizable."

In *Eager to Learn*, the authors pay particular attention to grading as a major contributor to students' declining motivation to learn.

Toddlers do not face this reality. No one would ever think of improving a poorly enunciated "da-da" by grading it. Imagine what might happen to the joy of cooking if the recipients of a meal graded it upon each occasion. "Your roast beef is only about a C, but don't worry; your gravy deserves a B. However, if I compare it with your neighbor's cooking, I'll have to lower the entire meal by half a grade." Sounds ridiculous doesn't it? Yet most children face this kind of thinking in their daily school lives. Grading does little to sustain a deeply felt desire for learning for the sake of learning.

A second diminisher of the motivation to learn is the increasing complexity of learning. Let's take a simple example. A first or second grader is praised for being able to spell and use a word correctly. The fact that other words are misspelled or that the subject and verb of the sentence in which the word is used do not agree is incidental. The child got the idea of the lesson. But as students move along in their schooling, subjects require more of them, and teachers are increasingly less forgiving of errors. For many, the journey into the area of advanced knowledge reaches a point of diminishing returns. Self-esteem falls victim to the process, as failures seem to outpace victories.

John O'Connor, North Dakota's Teacher of the Year, sees a lot of failure in the faces of his ninth-grade science students. He suggested to us that one of his roles as a teacher is to "get kids to open doors that were slammed on them earlier. They learn to accept failure and the labeling that goes along with it. And because of that, they don't ask questions, they don't take risks."

Finally, the desire to learn is sabotaged by the enormous attractions and distractions of a busy, exciting, and often chaotic world. As the young person's world widens, the environment offers ever more powerful choices that compete for time, energy, and attention. The motivation to learn, which dominated the life of the preschooler, now must compete with the motivation to be accepted, to earn some spending money, to acquire certain key possessions, and so on.

Theresa Noonan, Florida's Teacher of the Year, knows how compelling some of these things are to 12-year-olds and what stiff competition they give the teacher. Not invincible competition, however: "I really feel that one of the most important things that you must have in a class is 'fun.' When these kids are at home and can turn on MTV, and they have computer and video games and all of the other forms of entertainment, and then they go into traditional lecture-style instruction in a classroom, we lose them—it's not relevant, it's boring."

Besides the attractions over which kids have control, there are the distractions over which some of them have none. In rural communities, there are chores to be done. In large families, the older children may have to act as surrogate parents for the younger ones while both parents are out working. Latchkey kids may have the responsibilities of going shopping and starting dinner. Increasingly, children are aware of, and part of, problems that may afflict their parents' relationship—alcoholism, drug use, depression, physical or psychological abuse, the trials of separation and divorce.

How can a teacher hope to compete for attention when the child's family is falling apart? When responsibilities at home leave no energy for homework? When, in some inner-city schools, pupils fear for their lives? Is it reasonable to expect that a teacher can make a difference under such circumstances?

Certainly no one can be forced to learn, especially a distracted or unmotivated kid. Threats have minimal short-term effect and virtually no long-term effect. Poor grades are not a very good motivator either.

The motivation to learn must come from within, and teaching, according to the expert teachers we talked to, must be something that is done *with* and *for* students, not *to* them. Student and teacher should form a partnership in learning not unlike a joint venture in business, the buddy system in scuba diving, the mixed pairs in figure skating, or the relationship between Batman and Robin—a "dynamic duo."

The teacher as teacher is eminently forgettable, whereas the teacher as companion on a journey is a lifelong friend, as evidenced by the words of Robert Coles in the September 1990 issue of *Instructor*. The renowned author and professor of psychiatry at Harvard University had been asked to write about teachers who made a difference in his life, one of whom was Henry Gardner.

Children's Hours

The following shows how school-age children in the United States spend their time, in hours per week. The first column represents primary school and the second senior high school.

Household work	2.7	4.8
School work	27.0	30.0
In school	25.2	26.2
At home	1.8	3.8
Reading	0.9	1.6
Watching television	15.6	14.2
Playing games and sports	15.0	7.0
Sleeping	68.2	60.3

Source: Institute for Social Research, University of Michigan, 1990.

Possessions

Teens spent $55-billion in 1988, and some of them have a lot to show for it. The number of teens who own cars increased fivefold between 1968 and 1988. The following shows the percentage of 13- to 19-year-old girls who own the listed possessions.

Camera	85%
Stereo	70
Tape recorder	45
Tennis racket	26
VCR	16
Motor scooter	12
Stocks/bonds	12
Golf clubs	5

Source: NEA Today, December 1989, p. 26.

Later [in my schooling] came a Latin and Greek teacher, Henry Gardner, then a somewhat elderly man, as we saw it (only a few years older than I now am!) who could all of a sudden turn into one of Caesar's lieutenants, or a fierce Greek warrior. He was dramatic, yes, but such a characterization is all too simplistic; he was a teacher whose heart and soul were given to the classics, and who yearned for company in that regard.

. . .We were won over to him, by him, on that account—the respect he showed us by the desire he revealed to us that we be company to him in his imagination, fellow Roman and Greek soldiers. *Milites Romani,* he addressed us, Roman soldiers, or the equivalent in Greek.

It was a summons, an arousal, and of course, a call to arms in several senses—that we be mindful of the high stakes involved in that classroom activity: a foe to be vanquished when we conjugated a verb correctly or 'compared' an adjective and adverb accurately.

The partnership was complete, according to Coles, because "He gave us a kind of pride—not the unseemly sort that is unearned or gratuitous, but the kind we obtained through the sweat he asked us to expend on our class work, our homework, a sweat he so obviously more than matched on his own part."

Fast forward three decades to a performing arts class in Chicago. Students are arrayed around a piano, singing sixteenth-century madrigals, communicating to one another in short, lyrical phrases. The teacher, Bill Wilson, and his class are featured on the television program "Who's Minding the Kids? The Truth About Teachers."

"My energy comes from just being excited about what I'm doing," he says. The camera shifts from the students to a huge, multi-colored banner that nearly covers one wall of the room. It reads, NOTHING GREAT WAS EVER ACCOMPLISHED WITHOUT ENTHUSIASM.

Wilson obviously believes this message: "If I get excited about it, they are excited about it. I don't care what we are learning. When I get excited and run off and just go on, they just run with me. You can't fool them. They know when you are genuinely hooked on something."

The kind of zeal we are speaking of has no specific form or content. It is of no single style. Teachers must find within themselves their own source of excitement in teaching and learning and be willing to express it openly. That expression, the manifestation of the fire that burns within, can take as many different forms as there are teachers. As described by John Roueche and George Baker in *Profiling Excellence in America's Schools*, "One may be a formal, dignified teacher of English who quietly exhibits a deep appreciation of literature and draws a similar appreciation from his or her students. Another may be a 'fired up,' and often funny, math teacher who thinks first-year algebra is the greatest thing that ever happened."

The Zezulkas, the O'Connors, the Noonans—the teachers who can muster the Milites Romani and immerse their students in madrigals—have the remarkable ability to cut through youthful attractions and distractions, throwing themselves into their topic with abandon. They excite the intellect and inspire students to direct their energies to the subject at hand. They work with a fervor that challenges young people to wonder and reason, to explore and imagine. The irrepressible curiosity of the 2-year-old is recaptured daily in their classrooms.

12

Easier Said Than Done

"First of all, I am a hard worker."
—Geraldine Hawes
Tennessee Teacher of the Year

Everyone knows that teaching is easy work. The day is short, the vacations long, and the demands minimal. Anyone can do it, right? George Bernard Shaw probably precipitated this notion when he penned the teacher-basher's anthem, "He who can, does. He who cannot, teaches," and this fallacious view is still held by many people today.

Let's take a look at some of the hidden assumptions behind this view. The fact that the vast majority of the nation's teachers are women goes a long way toward explaining the myth that teaching is easy. It is an unfortunate fact that until very recently the common "wisdom" held that men did the difficult and important things, while women did simple, less challenging work. Men controlled the destinies of corporations, while women scurried after them, taking memos and dispensing coffee. Women in funny little hats dutifully took temperatures and blood pressure readings, while men performed brain surgery and saved lives. Men donned hard hats and went off to build roads and bridges—making the country great—while their wives stayed home washing clothes, cooking meals, and raising children. Women who weren't nurses, secretaries, or housewives were often teachers, an occupation that was neatly stereotyped with other "female" work as being necessary but not particularly demanding.

"Many *of the education courses that we are taught stink. I can't tell you how many I haven't used.*"

Another reason for the common perception that teaching is simple work is the relative ease of entry into the field. While a college degree is necessary, the schooling required for teacher certification ranks well below that for medicine, law, and engineering. Whereas the courses designed to prepare physicians and lawyers are usually viewed as difficult and necessary, most education courses are seen as less than demanding and not particularly germane to the act of teaching. Indeed, in *Teachers for Our Nation's Schools* John Goodlad reports that teachers find education courses impractical and Mickey Mouse. One of our Teachers of the Year, Len DeAngelis, went so far as to say, "Many of the education courses that we are taught stink. I can't tell you how many I haven't used."

The current national trend toward making certification available through means other than a college or university teacher-education program, while it has increased the supply of teachers in math and science and other subject areas with critical shortages, just exacerbates the problem. Imagine, for instance, what would happen to the considerable prestige in which people hold the medical profession if requirements for entry were relaxed.

The final reason people think teaching is easy is that most of them think they can do it. The general public has seen teachers "at work" more than any other occupational group. It's unusual to see an architect or surgeon at work, but for thirteen years—13,000 hours—the general public has grown up in classrooms and seen teachers at work. This familiarity demystifies teaching and leads to the belief that it is easy to do.

So much for perceptions. Let's take a look at the real world of teaching. The average teacher spends from 35 to 40 hours a week fulfilling his or her employment contract, but a teacher's routine, unlike that of other professionals, does not allow for coffee breaks, leisurely lunches, chats with colleagues around the watercooler, or moments of quiet contemplation.

Following is a quick glimpse of a typical teacher's workday, taken from the November 14, 1988, issue of *Time:* "Most weekdays, Juan Rodriquez, 46, roars up to Hartford's Thomas J. Quirk Middle School in his red pickup truck at 7 a.m. and leaves by 3 p.m." Your basic 40-hour work week. But that's where the similarity ends. "In between, he teaches five science classes, grades papers, prepares lesson plans, has two rounds of hall duty, grabs a sandwich at his desk and calls parents to discuss discipline problems or schoolwork." And that's not all. "The daytime schedule—which is often followed by two hours of work at home—sounds hectic, and it is. When the last-period bell rang on a recent afternoon, Rodriquez had not yet had an opportunity to go to the bathroom."

Effective teaching is no 40-hour-a-week enterprise. The National Education Association reports an average work week of 47.4 hours, with some teachers clocking as many as 60 hours. Why? Because good teachers are thinking constantly about their classrooms, their instructional approaches, their lesson plans. For example, here's the mental routine that Mercedes Bonner, Texas Teacher of the Year, goes through on a weekly basis.

> As I plan each week, I approach the lessons as if I am the learner. A series of questions enter my mind: When will I get confused about a concept? What experience will help me understand the idea? How can it be demonstrated or dramatized? How much will I absorb within a mental time block? When should a change of pace be in order? What materials do I need to make the lesson interesting? When will I get bored? When can I add bits of information? How can the week's work be balanced? Will I be challenged to think critically and creatively? What variety of teaching techniques will help me remember and enjoy the assignment? When would I like to be rewarded or praised for doing a good job?

"*E*nergy, enthusiasm, and a strong work ethic are necessary qualities for a teacher. "

Preparing lesson plans is just one of the things that extends the 40-hour work week. Teachers also may spend hours supervising after-school activities, providing extra help for students, conferring with parents, attending workshops, or serving on school committees.

Geraldine Hawes teaches high school English, drama, and speech in Tennessee. "I find that I spend many hours beyond the mandatory school day," she says. "Anyone who works with students in the performing arts knows about midnight set building, 7:30 a.m. rehearsals for contest speakers, weeks of 3:30-to-6:30 simulations for Model United Nations, and the many weekends spent preparing programs and tally sheets for the Toastmasters meetings." Hawes continues, "The term 'hard worker' may be trite, but energy, enthusiasm, and a strong work ethic are necessary qualities for a teacher."

Strong work ethic? Consider Jolanda Cannon's initiation into teaching. After a period as long-term substitute teacher for a sixth-grade class that met in a Quonset hut without air-conditioning in Broward County, Florida, she took her first full-time job teaching fourth-, fifth-, and sixth-grade reading, spelling, writing, and art in West Virginia. The school building had been condemned in 1920 but was still in use. Her smallest class had 37 students, the largest almost 50. "There weren't enough desks, so the students carried folding chairs from room to room. I had fifteen different reading groups a day, five for each grade," she recalls. There was no playground, just the street. "We had no cafeteria, so we walked several blocks to the high school in any and all kinds of weather." Somehow she and the children survived, and in 1990 she was chosen West Virginia Teacher of the Year.

Cannon now teaches in another school district where the working conditions are better—but not the work load—and she likes that just fine. "I'm just as busy now as I was then, because, being more experienced, I'm doing many more varied programs with students." She typically puts in a 9-hour day at school, including one 25-minute planning period and a half-hour lunch break—"7:30 to 3 is my scheduled day, but I'm the first one there and the last one to leave, at 4:30 on the average."

Cannon also devotes two evenings a week to school-related activities. Among her additional responsibilities are being the teacher representative on the school's PTA executive committee, serving as the school's building representative for the education association, running the school store, serving on the school improvement committee and the county staff development commit-

"Another rough day?"

Reprinted by permission of the artist.

"*T*he verb 'teach' may have every other verb in the dictionary as a synonym. "

tee, codirecting the county teachers' academy, and sitting on the advisory council for the county library. And she is also the substitute principal when the boss is away. Although she loves her job, she does admit that "when I come home on a Friday night, I don't want anything but a hot cup of tea and bed."

So teaching is no soft job, whether in terms of the hours or the work itself. In *Schoolteacher,* Dan Lortie gives an excellent description of a teacher's job as combining aspects of three other professions—the theater arts, business management, and psychotherapy. What makes teaching so difficult to do well is that, while it incorporates all the duties and responsibilities of these professions, it has numerous constraints they do not have.

First, a teacher is director, stage manager, actor, and even playwright. "The teacher," writes Lortie, "typically works alone and is forced to play all these roles simultaneously." While a theatrical production usually has someone responsible for assembling the props and paraphernalia necessary for engaging the audience's attention, "the teacher, on the other hand, works under comparatively humdrum conditions, with fewer resources for riveting attention." The teacher's audience is not there voluntarily, and "the teacher has less control over the situation than those directing theatrical productions."

Further, unlike directors, who can reject a script, teachers are often forced to follow a curriculum they have no control over. "Nor is the classroom a stage over which the teacher can legitimately assert full authority," since what goes on there is subject to review by higher authorities." And, we might add, the teacher's production changes every day, with no rehearsals and no rewrites.

Second, in Lortie's scheme, teachers function much like business managers in that "both set goals for groups of subordinates and try to lead them toward accomplishment. Both must decide how to allocate time and other scarce resources to get work done. Both must balance task and socioemotional considerations. Both distribute rewards and punishments to those in their charge." However, teachers must function without the budgetary and administrative authority normally accorded to business managers, and, perhaps because their subordinates are children, teachers do not enjoy the status of managers. Finally, their subordinates do not apply for their positions, cannot leave, and cannot be terminated for poor performance.

Like psychotherapists, teachers are expected to make judgments about people and prescribe remedies for the problems they perceive. "But although the tasks and imperatives may be similar for teachers and therapists," Lortie suggests, "there is normally a large difference in their prestige. Therapists may be licensed psychologists or physicians; where that is so, their claims to trust are buttressed by impressive qualifications based on protracted study." Teachers seldom enjoy that degree of trust or prestige.

So this "easy" job involves being a director and actor without the necessary controls and resources, a business manager without the power and status, and a psychotherapist without the formal recognition and support. To these we can easily add others—a parent without the authority, a substance-abuse counselor without the technical training, a cop without a badge.

Yet the best teachers thrive in these multifaceted and often unappreciated roles. They stretch themselves far beyond the narrow job descriptions that are part of most organizations. And they do it on a daily basis. "The totally involved teacher advises, coaches, assists, chaperones, and participates in as many facets of the profession as he or she can," says Len DeAngelis. "The verb 'teach' may have every other verb in the dictionary as a synonym. When one teaches well, one does a little of everything: laugh, cry, act, write, live, die—the list is endless."

13

The Legacy of Larry Glass

*"I want to spend my working years opening
doors to possibilities, dreams, and ideas
for young people."*
—Ann Haley-Oliphant
Ohio Teacher of the Year

"It would be a lot easier in the classroom if I could give up this . . .
part-time job," says Leonard Stanziano as he stocks convenience-
store shelves with cold beer. "There's no use complaining, because
I want to be a teacher, and I want to have children, so this is what
we're going to have to do."

Stanziano, a second-year teacher at Tom's River High School in
New Jersey, was featured in the NBC White Paper, *To Be a Teacher.*
"My salary at Tom's River comes to about $25,000 a year, with a
family, three kids, and one on the way. How do I feel about that?
Well, you only go through this life once, and if you can't do any
good what good are you?" Someone calls through the intercom,
"Lenny, can I have a cold case of Bud bottles, please?" Stanziano
concludes, "and that's why I'm probably going to stay in it, hope-
fully."

There is something terribly ironic about this scene. A mere 30
seconds of film highlight the extremes of contradiction in our view
of the teaching profession: on the one hand, it is worthy of the
special attention a televised report implies; on the other, Leonard
Stanziano is hauling cases of Budweiser. Why the disparity?

Everyone, from President Bush on down, agrees that the coun-

The "stock" of teachers is solid and surging.

try needs a great educational system. Politicians recognize that a representative form of government such as ours requires a well-informed, literate population to function. Businesspeople know that America's ability to compete in the new global economy is dependent upon our having an educated work force. Apparently, even Hollywood agrees. In 1990, the Disney Channel presented the American Teacher Awards, an inspirational tribute to thirty-six teachers from across the country, complete with celebrity hosts and cash awards to teachers and their schools totaling $250,000 in twelve categories.

Also in the profession's favor is the fact that the demand for teachers in this country is generally strong, although uneven. For example, mathematics and science teachers are desperately needed, while budget problems are causing some school districts to make serious across-the-board cuts. According to the National Center for Education Statistics, by 1997 we may need as many as 1.4 million new teachers.

The demand is being propelled by two main forces. First, the "baby echo"—children and grandchildren of the postwar baby boomers reaching school age—added to the influx of children of immigrant families in some areas of the country means that school enrollments are up substantially. At the same time, the National Education Association estimates that between 30 and 50 percent of the nation's teaching force will retire between 1990 and 1995.

In sum, education is recognized as being essential to the economic and social well-being of this country. Industry, the citizenry, and the political sector speak as one on the issue. Awareness of and interest in education is sky high. Further, demographics and the "graying" of the teaching population have conspired to produce a demand curve that resembles a Wall Street bull-market rally—the "stock" of teachers is solid and surging.

Anyone who has taken a basic economics course knows that the factors just outlined should create rising salaries and significantly better working conditions as school districts compete for new teachers. And salaries are up somewhat—the average teaching salary is around $33,000, ranging from South Dakota's $22,400 to Alaska's $43,900. Working conditions have improved in many schools as well. But demand is only half of the economic equation. What about supply?

If there were a shortage of doctors in this country, what would happen? Doctors' salaries would increase, perks would improve, the competition would heat up, and the marketplace would respond. Stories would appear in newspapers and on television: "The Doctor Is OUT!" or "Exposé: America's Declining Health Professionals." Parents would urge their children to be doctors when they grow up. Special doctor-shortage committees would be formed. Eventually the lure of inflated salaries and prestige would have the desired effect and attract the cream of the crop into the profession. Education, however, does not work that way. We have always chosen to secure an adequate number of teachers *by making it easy to become a teacher,* not with money or increased status.

States normally grant teaching certificates only after a candidate has taken a required number of education courses in college and has successfully completed a term of supervised practice teaching. However, during past teacher shortages states and local school districts have handled the problem by granting emergency credentials and by allowing certified teachers to teach outside their area of training. Such practices continue. For example, the New Hampshire State Board of Education recently adopted a plan that allows college graduates with a grade point average of at least 2.5 to teach subjects in which they have 30 credit hours *without any teacher training.* New York City employs 15,000 uncertified teachers. In some schools, usually elementary schools, as many as half the staff are unqualified to teach, not having met licensing requirements.

By manipulating licensing requirements or increasing class

"*Making sure that we had enough teachers has taken precedence over making sure that we had good ones.*"

sizes or the number of classes taught, states and school districts can easily alter the supply of teachers. But these practices, besides confusing the issue, mask the critical distinction between "covering classes" and "competent teaching." As John Goodlad writes in *Teachers for Our Nation's Schools,* "Throughout the history of our public education system, making sure that we had enough teachers has taken precedence over making sure that we had good ones."

What, then, drives the good ones? It isn't money. It isn't the desire to rise above the politics of boards of education and legislatures. It isn't the hope that they will win one of Disney's cash awards or make the network news. None of these things can begin to explain the motivation of great teachers or the existence of great classrooms. What is it that makes Leonard Stanziano run?

The teachers who are making a difference in America's classrooms have a streak of uncompromising idealism a mile wide. They want to be paid according to their worth to society. They want their profession to have high standards. But most of all, as individuals, they want to make a difference in the lives of young people.

Bill Nave told us, "While a premed undergraduate at Columbia University, I did volunteer work with ghetto youth at a nearby church. In so doing, I discovered that I had a gift for communicating with these young people. I also discovered that they were being written off by everyone in their lives—parents, teachers, peers, and, indeed, all of society. I was indignant."

Bill never made it to med school. "I decided to work with disadvantaged youth as a career, so after graduating I spent a summer

92

taking education credits at NYU. In September I began teaching at the largest ghetto middle school in New York City. It was like coming home. This was where I belonged."

Vermont's David Ely also talked about making a difference. As one of eighteen children from a poor, rural Vermont family, he was aware that "teachers made the difference in my life." He explained how "a couple of science teachers really gave me the chance to succeed at something, and I've never forgotten that. So I try, in any way that I can, to make a difference for other kids."

Molly Mueller Hankins, Missouri's Teacher of the Year, said, "I will always remember sitting in my eighth-grade social studies class when my teacher, Larry Glass, picked up a copy of *Exodus* by Leon Uris. He read to us an account of the atrocities at Auschwitz and Treblinka, atrocities his relatives had suffered." She continued, "I knew two things: that every individual had the obligation to educate himself and others to prevent future atrocities and that I wanted to be a part of that education process and to someday have the same impact on a student that Mr. Glass had had on me."

Leonard Stanziano's part-time job is an unfortunate byproduct of the numerous conflicting forces that tug and pull at the teaching profession. In the rush to place warm bodies in front of classes, we are losing sight of the need to improve the stature, working conditions, and financial security of teachers. But the Naves, Elys, and Hankinses ply their trade undeterred, carrying on in the legacy of Larry Glass, and there is reason to believe that the next generation of Teachers of the Year has already heard the call.

The author of a *New York Times* article on tomorrow's teachers (August 27, 1990) suggests that the widespread publicity regarding the crisis in education has tapped a new vein of idealism in the country. One young woman, an education major at Illinois State, is quoted as saying, "I've always done very well in school, so my father wanted me to go to law school or be a doctor or go into computers. For me, when I look into the future, I don't necessarily see computers but children, the best future that we have."

14

Spinning Plates

"Organization sets the tone."
—Nina Fue
New Jersey Teacher of the Year

You've seen the act—the performer places a plate on a long, thin pole and rotates it vigorously. The plate begins to spin around on the tip of the pole. The performer then runs to the next pole and starts the next plate in motion and then starts the next plate on the next pole and so on. After a while, the first plates have almost stopped spinning; wobbling grotesquely, they seem about to crash to the floor. The audience lets out a collective gasp. Just in the nick of time, the performer dashes back and gives the poles a quick spin, the plates right themselves, and the sweating, wild-eyed balancer scrambles back to set more plates in motion. This frantic act continues, teetering between triumph and disaster, until all plates are spinning, neatly balanced on their thin shafts.

What does the seemingly maniacal performance of the plate-balancer have to do with the best classrooms in the nation? Like these entertainers, good teachers must balance the variety of demands placed on them in the course of a day and keep all the plates spinning. In a 1987 survey of 22,000 public school teachers, the Carnegie Foundation found that, while teaching is becoming increasingly complicated, the conditions under which teachers work often frustrate them and reduce their effectiveness. They are faced with too many students, too much paperwork, too many interrup-

"*A* lack of organization breeds disorder and invites frustration. "

tions in the classroom, and too little time for preparation—in effect, too many spinning plates.

What is the solution? The American Association of School Administrators recently published a booklet that summarizes findings about the techniques and characteristics of effective teachers. It suggests that *effective teachers tend to be good managers*. This means mastering three key elements of classroom dynamics: time, space, and people.

Researchers have found that average daily academic learning time—the time students actually spend engaged in learning—is often less than 2 hours, or about 40 percent of their time in class. Students in the classes of ineffective teachers tend to average about 30 minutes less, while those in the classes of effective teachers average about 30 minutes more. This 60-minute difference means that over the school year an effective teacher is able to give students 180 hours' more instruction than an ineffective one, in theory extending the school year by thirty-six days.

Fundamental to teachers' increasing their "time on task" is simply knowing where they are going. This ability to define clearly a set of intended outcomes was described to us by Connecticut's Chaz Zezulka: "If we want our lessons to be understood, to be internalized, to be remembered, we should provide our students with a framework for enhancing learning. Students need to understand why a certain skill or idea is presented to them. By drawing students' attention to our objectives at the beginning of a lesson, throughout the lesson, and at the end, we help them to focus on key things to learn."

Good teachers also have a detailed plan for reaching their destination. They know *which* teaching materials will be used and *how* they will be used. This has many benefits. As Mercedes Bonner put it, "When students see an organized planner and thinker, they feel confident in what is expected of them. A lack of organization breeds disorder and invites frustration."

The best teachers employ a systematic and businesslike approach to their classroom activities, which is not to say that they are rigid. They are acutely attuned to how well things are going and to unique learning opportunities that may arise. If the planned activity is not working, they can switch to a backup before the students are lost to boredom, frustration, or confusion. As Roueche and Baker note in *Profiling Excellence in America's Schools*, "Even with a plan, effective teachers remain flexible. Plans are not written in stone; and if the unexpected occurs—a spontaneous discussion, an unannounced fire drill, a triumph or tragedy in the class—the teacher incorporates that occurrence into the plan and adjusts."

Demonstrating another facet of being orderly without rigidity, the best teachers always seem to know what time it is. They have a built-in timepiece that allows them to pace their lessons without having to look at the classroom clock. They seem to know instinc-

══ Teachers as Managers ══

Many researchers have focused on classroom management as an important component of effective teaching. A well-organized classroom where a minimum of time is spent in maintaining discipline, making transitions between classes and repeating instructions, helps to increase the amount of time available for instruction and—ideally—the actual time spent learning. Up to a certain point, when learning time is used effectively student performance increases. . . . Although management and instruction are [usually] discussed separately, in practice the two are irrevocably intertwined. The key management elements—increasing the time available for learning, preventing disruptions, and keeping students profitably engaged in quality activities—are a vital part of effective teaching.

Source: American Association of School Administrators, *Effective Teaching: Observations from Research* (Arlington, Va.: 1986), p. 5.

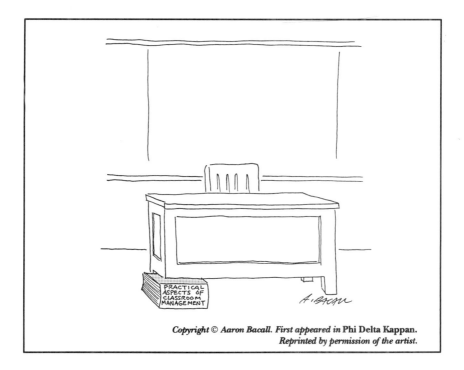

Copyright © Aaron Bacall. First appeared in Phi Delta Kappan.
Reprinted by permission of the artist.

tively how far into a lesson they are and how much time is left. They know when to slow down to stress crucial points and when to speed up to keep the kids' interest alive. Because they have the ability to adjust quickly when lessons are not moving at a productive rate, teachers have been called "opportunistic planners." Put another way, they know when the plates are starting to wobble.

A side benefit of effective time management has to do with discipline. Florida's Theresa Noonan, a wily veteran of the classroom, put it so well: "If we do become better managers of time, we can eliminate 90 percent of all discipline problems. Discipline problems occur because you've lost the kids—they're not interested anymore because they don't understand, they tune you out—and second of all, they have time on their hands with nothing to do." She concluded, "If we manage the time more effectively, not only will learning increase and improve but also discipline problems just disappear."

In addition to being good time managers, effective teachers are also good at managing space. If you have ever been to a Broadway show, you have witnessed the value of this kind of management. Every night and twice on Sundays and Wednesdays, dozens of actors, dancers, and singers must "hit their marks" and be in a specific place at a specific time. The swords must be in the right spot for the fight scene; the lights must be ready to follow the action; the chairs and tables need to be properly positioned so that the dancers have room to complete their turns and twists; the music must be loud enough but not so loud as to drown out the singers' voices. When the stage manager has done the job correctly, the result is a smooth-running, highly polished presentation that makes the costly tickets worth every penny.

The really good teachers visualize their classrooms as stages. In order for students and teacher to hit their marks, the physical arrangement of the classroom must be stage-managed actively. Perceptive teachers make sure that all the necessary materials are close at hand and in sufficient quantity and that desks and tables are arranged to maximize learning objectives. They are aware of spatial relationships, avoiding congestion in heavily used areas and ensuring chalkboard visibility for everyone. They use positive images and symbols to reinforce achievement and are aware of how lighting, color, texture, and sound can influence attitudes and behaviors.

Unfortunately, most teacher-training programs, while they emphasize philosophies of education, theories of instruction, curriculum methods, and class materials, devote little time to the integral importance of the physical environment in the learning experience. The manner in which we organize our classroom environments says a lot to children about how we feel about them, how we think they learn, and how we expect them to learn. As Paula Jorde has suggested in a marvelous book, *Avoiding Burnout: Strategies for Managing Time, Space, and People in Early Childhood Education*,

"The physical environment needs to be stimulating and inviting to all students. **"**

"In many respects, our arrangement of space serves as a kind of *hidden curriculum,* relaying powerful messages to children about our expectations for their behavior."

Chaz Zezulka comes at the same thing from his own perspective: "The physical environment needs to be stimulating and inviting to all students. The classroom can provide students with a sense of connectedness, of belonging, if they are allowed to become a part of the learning environment."

An example of a well-managed learning environment with a hidden curriculum is described in *Voices from the Classroom: Exceptional Teachers Speak,* a report that summarizes the views of 115 extraordinary teachers from across the country. The classroom of a high school science teacher from Chapel Hill, North Carolina, "replete with snakes, lizards, rodents, insects and aquatic creatures, is a place where students congregate in their free time before school, after school and during lunch. They hold animals, eagerly clean the cages and borrow books from her extensive personal library." According to the teacher, she tries to create an environment in her classroom that "invites students into the mysteries and excitement of learning biology."

When it comes to people management, every teacher develops his or her own style, but there are a few things that seem to be common in all effective classrooms. First, good teachers take control from day one. They establish rules and routines early on in the school year and then—and this is the most important part—actively and consistently follow them up.

Debbie Pace Silver has procedures for taking attendance, collecting homework, arranging for students to make up work after

100

absences, setting up and using laboratory equipment, and sharpening pencils. The effect is to keep distractions to an absolute minimum. As Nina Fue suggested to us, this allows the teacher to "hit a rhythm." Her fourth-grade students work in many groups on a variety of activities, which means that a lot of different things are happening simultaneously. To keep this from turning into complete chaos, she establishes procedures early in the year and then reinforces them, monitoring and providing corrective feedback. After the kids get the routine, it all works smoothly.

A second feature of successful people management is modeling. As Roueche and Baker point out in *Profiling Excellence in America's Schools,* "effective teachers model the behaviors they expect. They are punctual, well organized, and do not waste time. They stay on task, are businesslike and do not interrupt the learning task. . . . They are friendly and attentive to individual needs, and make it clear that they expect a like behavior from the students."

Kids of all ages are keenly aware of hypocrisy. They resent, and rightly so, teachers who ask more of their students than they demand of themselves. Teachers cannot expect students to be responsible, organized, and disciplined if they themselves are late in returning work, messy, or unprepared.

Knowing all these things is a good start, but it takes time, experience, and some risk-taking to get organized. The rookie teacher will have to learn quite a few painful lessons before things start to smooth out. When we were discussing our spinning plate analogy with Wisconsin's Teacher of the Year Lee Schmitt, he remarked, "But you know, we see that act *after* the fellow has perfected his routine. He didn't start out being able to keep twenty going at once. In fact, he probably smashed a hundred plates before he got through the first day. Until you get the procedure down, and that takes patience and energy, you are necessarily going to be doing a lot of cleaning up."

15

Weekday Warriors

*"I've been engaged in a never-ending
battle. . . . "*
—Theresa Noonan
Florida Teacher of the Year

Who are the "customers" in our education system? The parents of school-aged children? How about the school boards, superintendents, and principals who set the rules and regulations? Perhaps the legislators who allocate the funding for education? Maybe the industries that employ the graduates of our schools? A democracy requires an educated citizenry to function, so perhaps society as a whole is the customer. While all these groups have a vested interest in the schools' well-being, it would be a mistake to call them customers. Stakeholders, yes; beneficiaries and patrons, absolutely. But *the real customer in the education system is the student.*

The consumer in our education system, the one Theresa Noonan is battling for, is the kid in the third row with the Bart Simpson T-shirt and the confused look. This person's needs should come first—not industry's, not the principal's, not the superintendent's, not even the parents'. Effective teachers are advocates for students and are willing to speak loud and long to guarantee the right of each child to a high-quality education in a student-centered system. A recent report, *Voices from the Classroom: Exceptional Teachers Speak*, states unequivocally, "A common attribute of exceptional teachers tends to be assertiveness. From all that they report about themselves, they are ready and willing to act forcefully, if necessary, to get what they consider necessary for their students."

What's with the tough talk, and why this edge to advocacy? The reason is that many obstacles come between teachers and their responsibility to the students. First among these is bureaucracy.

In the movie *Dead Poets Society,* Robin Williams portrays Mr. Keating, a first-year literature teacher at Welton Academy. There is a "Welton way" of doing things, and no other way is tolerated. Within this rigid environment Williams's character challenges the students to think for themselves, act on their passions, dare to be different, seize the day—*carpe diem.*

Keating has the students rip out the introduction to their poetry books, in which the author offers a "formula" for evaluating poetry. "This is a battle. A war!" he shouts as they toss the pages into a trash can, "and the casualties could be your hearts and souls." In another scene, he has the boys huddle in the center of the room so he can tell them to "learn to think for yourselves. You must learn to savor words and language. Words and ideas can change the world." And then there is the scene in which he has them stand on the desk to illustrate how important it is to look at things differently. Keating believes passionately that he can make a difference in his boys' lives. But the administration of the academy is less concerned with meeting the needs of individual students than it is with perpetuating the status quo, and Keating's unorthodox style makes him the obvious scapegoat when things go badly wrong.

While this is only the movies, the plain fact is that schools are among society's most unbending institutions. Historically, they have tended to be static rather than changing and to value uniformity over diversity. This inevitably turns the day-to-day operations of dynamic, proactive teachers into a battle—a battle for creativity, change, and opportunity—a battle to keep the casualties among students' "hearts and souls" to a bare minimum.

Of course the administration of schools has changed greatly since the year the document on the facing page was posted. Most of today's teachers would not have the slightest idea of how to trim

Rules for Teachers

1. Teachers each day will fill lamps, clean chimneys and trim wicks.
2. Each teacher will bring a bucket of water and scuttle of coal for the day's sessions.
3. Make your pens carefully. You may whittle nibs to the individual tastes of the pupil.
4. Men teachers may take one evening each week for courting purposes or two evenings a week if they go to church regularly.
5. After ten hours of school, the teacher should spend the remaining time reading the Bible or other good books.
6. Women teachers who marry or engage in unseemly conduct will be dismissed.
7. Every teacher should lay aside from each pay a goodly sum of his earnings for his benefit during declining years, so that he will not be a burden on society.
8. Any teacher who smokes, uses liquor in any form, frequents pool or public halls or gets shaved in a barber shop will give good reason to suspect his worth, intentions, integrity, and honesty.
9. The teacher who performs his labors faithfully and without fault for five years will be given an increase of twenty-five cents per week in his pay, providing the Board of Education approves.

Posted by a principal
in New York City, 1872

"*T*he schools have become just another organization whose major focus is self-perpetuation."

their wicks or whittle their nibs. But take another look through the 1872 "Rules for Teachers" and compare them to the following list of desirable characteristics for teachers, as specified by superintendents and other administrators in a 1989 American Association of School Administrators' survey.

- Will follow school district policy
- Have a good work ethic
- Aren't in teaching for the money
- Can speak and write correctly
- Can take suggestions
- Are punctual
- Have good attendance records
- Can cope with students
- Will work beyond the school day
- Have high moral values
- Have common sense

One has to wonder how much things have changed when, for the most part, the people in charge still focus on how teachers relate to their supervisors rather than on how they relate to their students.

Maine's Bill Nave suggested to us that many schools have succumbed to a problem common to all human organizations: "They have lost sight of their real and original purpose and have become just another organization whose major focus is self-perpetuation. Schools must again begin to ask themselves the fundamental questions, 'How can we meet the real needs of our students?' and 'How can we best prepare our students to be productive citizens of the 1990s and beyond?'"

If institutional rigidity causes gifted teachers to be lost along the way, Bill Nave foresees a far greater loss for society: "If we are unable to succeed in the endeavor of reforming the schools to truly meet student needs, we will continue to lose the positive contributions of millions of individuals representing billions of dollars' worth of human resources, both in lost wages and taxes, and in increased social services costs."

Government and politicians often erroneously think that they—or the nation they represent—are the real customers of the education system. Carole Kasen, South Dakota's Teacher of the Year, is a child-centered teacher with a clear understanding of the power of politics and funding. She directs a series of programs for gifted and talented children. One of them is a summer camp for seventh, eighth, and ninth graders from around the state that provides leadership training and challenging work beyond the scope and resources of schools in many of the state's rural communities.

According to Kasen, "Several years ago a bill was introduced to remove the mandate for gifted education from under the 94142 Special Education Law . . . most states include gifted education under that umbrella." Once this protection was removed, her program became easy pickings for special interest groups with political agendas. "So, when we try to do things that are not standard or by a formula for the children, when we try to diverge from the curriculum and work for the child instead of whatever the administrative mandates are, we run into trouble."

To illustrate the point, Kasen told us about the Governor's Scholars Program: "Each year we need to lobby our friends in the legislature to set aside appropriations for various programs for the gifted. Our Governor's Scholars Program is funded in the governor's line item budget, and, this year, when it hit the appropriations committee, the scholarships for our rural and rural-isolated children were removed. We had a very small appropriation, one

"*We are always fighting for the extracurricular programs that make the classroom come alive.* "

that allows children with no funds to attend. We were able, through some good friends and some all-night lobbying, to restore $15,000—it provides $100 scholarships for 150 children."

Theresa Noonan tells a similar story: "We are always fighting for the extracurricular programs that make the classroom come alive. For example, whether it's a trip to Washington to study the government or a trip to the Florida Keys to study marine biology, administration traditionally approaches this rather conservatively, in that they don't want to take on the problems that accompany such activities. Teachers are more willing to take the risks, because we see the need to make the classroom come alive and be more relevant to these kids' lives."

She went on to tell us that "One of the first things they look to cut is what some people have traditionally thought of as frills, and most of the people who label these kinds of activities frills are legislators who have probably not stepped a foot in a classroom since they graduated. They are making the decision and don't really want to listen to the teachers. We are in a constant struggle to communicate effectively with those people who don't seem to want to hear us."

Both school bureaucracy and the politics of education tend to shift the spotlight of attention away from the student, making it difficult and at times impossible for a conscientious teacher to follow his or her instincts and training. The final problem student-centered teachers must fight to overcome is indifference to the kids and abandonment. It is essential that students know someone cares whether they succeed or not. The social and economic conditions facing today's young people are dispiriting—the demise of the traditional family, drugs, gangs, street violence, joblessness, homelessness. It is easy for them to give up. It is easy to give up on the kids and on their schools, and all too often the indifference is semi-official, institutionalizing society's expectation of their chances for success.

In the January 1990 issue of *New York Newsday* titled "Do the Kids Have a Chance?" the principal and teachers of one Brooklyn, New York, school received special attention because of their unwillingness to accept the failure others perceived to be inevitable. Alice Uzoaga, the longtime principal of PS 21, the Crispus Attucks School, described the general expectation for students, teachers, even the principal: "As long as you're not stealing money, or brought up on drug charges or sexual abuse, [the Board of Education] won't step in. That school can just stay like that forever." In contrast, pushing to think and be successful is a constant struggle: "Everything we get we are earning, through blood, sweat and tears." Yet children at PS 21 consistently learn to read and do math at least as well as children in schools in other sections of the country.

The odds against success may be high, the environment may be difficult and depressing, but these are not sufficient reasons for the staffers at PS 21 to throw in the towel.

> About 80 percent of the 570 students at PS 21 . . . are poor enough to qualify for free lunch, and an increasing number are being raised by their grandmothers because their parents are on crack. But PS 21's assistant principal, Renee Young, scoffs at schools that cite such family problems and poverty as reasons for poor academic performance. "What, we can only teach children who have two parents?" she asks. "We can only teach children who eat breakfast? We can only teach children whose parents are employed? That's ridiculous. That's a cop-out. That's not acceptable. We have no control over the homelife, but we have control over what happens now in school."

The excuses for discouragement, for low expectations, are plentiful. But in an environment in which "pupil learning is this school's top priority," somehow things manage to get accomplished.

"*Teaching is a people business, and you have to make a sacrifice for the students who are learning.* "

It would be difficult to imagine a place more removed from the streets of Brooklyn than Beaver Dam, Wisconsin. That's where Lee Schmitt, the state's Teacher of the Year, educates junior high school students in science. "I am a student-centered teacher. That is why I am in the classroom. And I'll do the paperwork and make contact with the administration. But the kids are number one."

Unlike the stark abandonment that typifies the lives of many kids in the projects of Brooklyn, indifference in Beaver Dam is more subtle. Lee Schmitt directs a science fair each year, a voluntary program in which 60 to 70 percent of the students get involved. The projects require a tremendous amount of time on the part of Schmitt and the participating students. A few years ago, "a student's parents decided to take a vacation for the week that we were doing our science fair. The student was in tears, because she had worked very hard on her project, and she wanted to be there and have the interview—and have a chance at a ribbon and perhaps go to the state competition.

"It took some doing, but I made special arrangements for her to talk with the people who were going to be the judges, to set up her project in advance, and I found a friend to watch the project and take it down—the inconveniences went on and on. She did not wind up with a ribbon and didn't go to the state competition. And, to be honest, the project was not fantastic. It was a good project, and she received a very good grade, but it was not competitive with the winners that year."

It would have been easy to stick to the rules and ignore the student's enthusiasm, but the weekday warriors of this book simply don't let that happen. Back to our story. . . . "She came up to me

110

afterwards and said, 'Why did you do it? Why did you go through all that hassle for me when you didn't have to?' I stopped for a second, because I hadn't realized I had done all this extra work. I said, 'It's my job'.... Teaching is a people business, and you have to make a sacrifice for the students who are learning. To tell you the truth, I never even thought about it. I probably spent six or seven hours just on that. I didn't win anything. I don't know," he laughed, "I'm thinking about this now and wondering, 'Why the heck did I do all that?' Because a light had gone on in her head. She's in college now, and a chemistry major." Ahh . . . the spoils of war.

16

When Will You Be Teaching?

"The role of teacher has changed from
lecturer to facilitator."

—Theresa Noonan
Florida Teacher of the Year

It was the day after James Ellingson had been interviewed by the local newspaper about being chosen Minnesota's Teacher of the Year. He was conducting a writing class, or Writers' Workshop, as he refers to it. Over in a corner of the classroom, two kids were reviewing each other's stories—"How does that sound?" one asked the other. Several children were at the dictionary, shuffling pages, looking up words. Some were huddled over the computers at the back of the room. Still others were seated quietly at tables putting pencil to paper.

As Ellingson was "conferencing" with a small group of students in another corner, a photographer from the local paper entered the classroom and asked, "You know that interview we did with you last night after school? We need some pictures to go along with it." Glancing around the activity-strewn classroom, the photographer added, "I can come back later. . . . When will you be teaching?"

According to the conventional view, teaching is something *done* by one person to one or more others in a direct transfer of knowledge or skill. For instance, James Ellingson went to college, where he studied, among other things, English composition and creative writing. He wrote term papers and short stories throughout his college career. He refined his writing skills in graduate school.

113

Over the years, he continued to study and experiment with various writing techniques and methods. He is an expert when it comes to writing.

It follows, in the common view, that what Ellingson should be doing is standing up in front of his eighth graders and telling them how to write—describing the conventions, dictating examples, assigning exercises, and administering quizzes and tests on the material he has covered. It's no wonder the photographer was confused—if that's teaching, not much of it appeared to be going on in Ellingson's classroom.

According to the authors of *Tomorrow's Teachers,* the traditional model equates teaching with presenting or passing on a substantive body of knowledge. Such a view assumes that "bright, well-educated individuals can draw on their accumulated knowledge to develop coherent, logical presentations which can be delivered and hence learned by students in orderly classrooms." The teacher's task is to develop and deliver a lesson; the student's is to learn that lesson. "The teacher's responsibility basically ends when they have told students what they must remember. . . . "

Many teachers seem to feel this makes good sense. In the National Center for Education Statistics' 1990 report, *Accelerating Academic Achievement,* national studies of instructional practices indicate that "one-way teaching" is the preferred method of instruction among an overwhelming majority of teachers. For example, 94 percent of eleventh-grade mathematics students said that they "listen to their teacher explain a lesson" during the week. Equal percentages of students "used a mathematics textbook" and "watched their teacher work problems on the board." Only 27 percent "worked problems in small groups," and less than 10 percent were asked to "make a report or do a project." U.S. history classes were even more skewed. Ninety percent of students said that they "read material from their textbook" during the week. Almost 80 percent "take a test or quiz." In contrast, just 15 percent "work on a group project."

If this is the tradition of American teaching, it is fortunate that

"*The teacher is not the sole source of knowledge but just another resource available to the child.*"

our Teachers of the Year are anything but traditional. Florida's Theresa Noonan commented to us, "We need to challenge some of these old beliefs, such as the notion of a principal walking into a classroom and everything is quiet, with students sitting there working in tight little rows—those days are gone."

In the most creative classrooms, the role of teacher as lecturer has changed to that of the teacher as facilitator. As Noonan went on to explain, "Students learn well from other students. In some of your more successful and effective classrooms, you will see students teaching. Teachers are going to give direction, initiate lessons, and provide the proper environment, but after that the kids are going to run with the ideas." Judith Crawford of New Mexico, another Teacher of the Year, agrees. In stark contrast to a "presenting" approach, she sees the teacher as a mediator or guide between the learner and the curriculum. "The teacher is not the sole source of knowledge but just another resource available to the child."

Wisconsin's Lee Schmitt gave us a good example of this facilitating approach, or "cooperative learning," as it has come to be called. "When I teach about the Kennedy years—let's say the Cuban missile crisis—most kids don't have a clue about what happened. I'll talk about the situation and ask them, 'What could the President have done?' We'll brainstorm and come up with all different options." The image of neat rows of stoic, tight-lipped kids begins to blur. Schmitt continued, "Then in groups they each take on roles of key figures—the president, Robert Kennedy, all of these different individuals—and they present their decisions to the class. We put a huge map in front of the room, project on it the ships headed in the direction of Cuba, and they talk about what they'd do and why." So much for one-way teaching.

The real payoff in Schmitt's approach to teaching the Cuban missile crisis has little to do with the direct transfer of knowledge from teacher to student. Dates and details are less important here than the subtle nudge being given to the thinking skills. "They don't know the outcome. They know we must have survived it okay because we are all here, but they don't know what happened. It's interesting to see what they come up with, their thought processes in working through the problem."

What may not be apparent is how much more difficult it is to be a facilitator rather than a presenter in terms of the preparation, planning, and implementation of a lesson. While James Ellingson's writing class may appear to be a disciplinarian's nightmare, the fact is that the lesson and group work are carefully orchestrated. Lee Schmitt explained that "you have to have your

Group Investigation

Shlomo Sharan of Tel-Aviv University has developed a very promising cooperative learning approach called Group Investigation.

1. Students identify subtopics within a broader topic for group study. The teacher divides the class into small groups, and each chooses a subtopic to work on.
2. Once in groups, students identify still smaller subtopics to work on as individuals or in pairs.
3. Students make and carry out plans for gathering information and exchanging it. They discuss ideas and problems, analyze their information, then decide how to combine their work into a single product.
4. Students prepare a group report and decide how to present it to the whole class—without giving a lecture.
5. Groups present their reports to the whole class, seeking maximum involvement of class members. They use skits, demonstrations, experiments, exhibitions, quiz shows.
6. The students evaluate the presentations of their own and other groups, using a variety of methods and points of view.

Source: Articles written or coauthored by Shlomo Sharan in *Children Helping Children* (Wiley, 1989) and *Cooperative Learning: Theory and Research* (Praeger, 1989).

groups set up correctly. You can't just throw four kids together and say 'You're a group.' They have to be heterogeneous groups—upper ability, lower ability, average ability. It doesn't do any good if you have all equal-ability kids at one table." From deciding who will be in each group to identifying desired learning outcomes, cooperative learning requires a well-articulated plan of action.

So the controlled chaos of Ellingson's, Noonan's, and Schmitt's classrooms is nontraditional. So group investigation flies in the face of one-way teaching. So what? That doesn't necessarily make it any better. In fact, it often may be inappropriate. But the best teachers want to have their tool kits full of varied techniques. Then, in doing their planning, they can trade off the strengths and weaknesses of each before deciding which delivery system is best for the circumstances. And group work seems to have so many strengths—the building of social relationships, the bashing of ethnic barriers, ownership of the educational experience and the consequent empowerment, preparation for the real world, enhanced learning outcomes, and just plain fun.

In Shlomo Sharan's research on the group investigation model described on the facing page, he used a combined measure of student motivation to assess its effectiveness. He found the following:

1. Students showed increased willingness to stay in class instead of going to recess.
2. Teachers were increasingly aware of student involvement in class.
3. Students were estimated to put greater effort into their homework than those taught by the "whole-class method."
4. Group investigation may have a positive influence on social relations in the classroom, which may, in turn, improve motivation.

Working in groups with students from different ethnic and cultural backgrounds also can be an enriching experience. In the

"I *truly believe that children are the most impotent and oppressed group in our society.* **"**

statement he submitted for consideration as Pennsylvania Teacher of the Year, Howard Selekman wrote the following:

> What more fundamental or humanitarian teaching could there be than getting students to learn that people help one another and that students of multi-cultural and ethnic diversity have a lot to learn together from one another? I will go so far as to say that homogeneous tracking in our schools has been a deterrent in helping our students feel a sense of unity and mutual dependence; rather it has built the walls higher and thicker.... It is our obligation to show our children that just as members of a family always try to be there for one another, support one another, solve problems with one another's help, so we can extend that nurturing to the concept of neighborhood, community, city, county, state, nation, and world. And for our students whose families of origin cannot supply those "family ties," then I say our schools must act as the student's extended family and help fill in the gaps. I believe that cooperative learning holds extraordinary promise for helping our students become successful citizens of a global community.

Another big advantage of a cooperative approach is the way it extends ownership of and responsibility for the learning process. In a presenting approach, the children are passive vessels, waiting to be filled. The teacher has a monopoly on knowledge, owning Boardwalk, Park Place, all the utilities, and most of the rest of the board. The kids are powerless. They never get a chance to pass "Go."

South Dakota's Carole Kasen puts the situation aptly: "I truly believe that children are the most impotent and oppressed group in our society. Many are sorely neglected—those of upper-income

118

families—and abandoned while their parents are climbing the ladder of success. Other kids are turned over to the schools for indoctrination of values and manners—and in some cases feeding and clothing." By bringing students into the learning process, she can give them a much-needed sense of responsibility and owner-ship. "I try to work with children in a way that not only expresses my compassion for their situation but in a way that will empower them to work through their own problems."

Not only does this approach do wonders for kids' sense of re-sponsibility and self-esteem, but it teaches them to get along with others—to share, to "network," to come together to work on com-mon problems—all desirable qualities when it comes to entering the world of work. As Maryland's Anne Neidhardt put it, "Students love to socialize with one another, and I capitalize on this interest by having them do learning activities in teams. Teamwork allows them to develop respect and trust in one another . . . become more cooperative and responsible." She added, "Teamwork helps to prepare them for the adult world, where most work is accom-plished by team effort."

There is also reason to believe that the cooperative classroom environment created by Kasen, Neidhardt, and the others has an impact on the bottom line—learning outcomes are improved. In Sharan's comparative studies, he found that students in classes using group investigation got higher scores in arithmetic and read-ing comprehension than did students whose class worked as a whole.

> **"***T****eamwork helps to prepare them for the adult world, where most work is accomplished by team effort.* **"**

119

If we accept the results contained in *Accelerating Academic Achievement,* instructional practices in most classrooms still follow the standard routine: (1) read the textbook, (2) listen to the teacher, and (3) take a quiz. This lock-step procedure may occasionally be interrupted by a video or a discussion, but the underlying pattern is always the same. Group work, on the other hand, reduces boredom, weariness, and discipline problems and produces excitement, energy, and fun. Stress levels go down and interest goes up as some variation on the read-listen-write model is introduced.

Many teachers act like production-line managers. Their classrooms are factories without the smokestacks. They see themselves as being paid to manage the neat little rows and generate results by transmitting information. And many people expect teachers to

"Pop quiz, I presume."

behave this way. It was the expectation of the photographer who entered James Ellingson's classroom. Her definition of teaching was decidedly one-way. Thank goodness, the best teachers think of the classroom as a busy intersection, the traffic of learning flowing in many directions at once.

17

The Einstein Factor

*"I love learning. I try to share that love of
learning with my students."*
—Barbara Firestone
Kansas Teacher of the Year

One of the most commonly called-for solutions to the country's education problems is to attract the nation's "best and brightest" into the classroom. This call has come on the heels of the teacher competence tests some states began giving in the mid-1980s. In Texas, for example, over 6,500 veteran teachers flunked a basic literacy test. Ten percent of Arkansas teachers failed a math, reading, and writing exam, while 12 percent of Georgia teachers failed exams in their specific disciplines. Currently the average teacher in training is from the middle or lower part of the high school class and has scored below the college-bound average on the Scholastic Aptitude Test.

To attract a better candidate pool to the teaching profession, some states have initiated scholarships or forgivable loans for bright young people who are willing to teach for a stipulated period of time. For example, North Carolina's Teaching Fellows Program recruits state residents in the top 10 percent of their high school classes. In exchange for a four-year commitment to teach in the state after graduation, the students receive free college tuition, room, and board.

To get "quality students involved in teaching," Wisconsin has instituted Teacher World, a summer camp for high school stu-

═══Teach for America═══

Teach for America, a national program that is beginning to gain attention, encourages the brightest college graduates to consider teaching. Back in 1988, her junior year at Princeton University, Wendy Kopp was at a conference in San Francisco with other college students, brainstorming ways to improve education. "Everyone was throwing out typical things—raise teachers' salaries and increase accountability," she says. She looked around her—students from Yale, Boston University, Emory, Berkeley—and realized that part of the answer was right there. Her idea—place college graduates with little or no teaching experience in classrooms, where they could discover the rewards and challenges of teaching. Top students would be lured by making the program exclusive, recruiting from the nation's most prestigious colleges, and putting recruits through a rigorous selection process. The result, she theorized, would be help for schools facing teacher shortages and a boost in the status of the profession—a sort of Peace Corps for teachers in inner-city and rural schools.

Kopp used her senior public policy thesis as an opportunity to develop an implementation plan, and, one year later, with the financial backing of some of the country's foremost companies and foundations, she launched Teach for America.

The process of selecting participants in the Teach for America program involves a written application, a sample teaching demonstration, and two interviews. Corps members then participate in an eight-week summer institute that focuses on cultural awareness and the acquisition of fundamental teaching skills, followed by two-year teaching assignments in rural schools and major urban centers. For the 1991–92 school year, Teach for America selected 700 corps members from 3,100 applications.

---

dents who are considering a teaching career. The Wisconsin Department of Public Instruction requests nominations from schools around the state. From these, 120 students are chosen to attend the camp, at which the focus is "teaching about teaching." Participants learn the ins and outs of the profession from some of the best teachers in the state and get a chance to try teaching for themselves.

While we certainly agree that America needs the "best" in its classrooms and applaud such innovative ideas, we are not sure about giving top priority to the "brightest." After all, does it really take a Ph.D. from Harvard to teach math to 12-year-olds? Although highly desirable, intellectual ability is just part of a set of equally important qualifications for a teacher

Tomorrow's Schools: Principles for the Design of Professional Development Schools states, "The kind of teaching we need does not require exceptionally brilliant or creative people. What is important is that teachers be engaged, that they observe their students, follow them closely, find out what excites them, and then help them to do that. You will know you have been successful if students leave school after ten or twelve years with a passion for something." Many readers probably can remember that college professor renowned for his "brilliance" who dazzled you with his knowledge yet also thoroughly confused you because he was incapable of making anything understandable.

The need to strike the right balance between intellectual ability and teaching ability was frequently mentioned in our conversations with teachers. Maryland's Arne Neidhardt feels that the "most academically successful" students can be "too self-focused to be successful teachers." To her, and to us, the kind of bright person that is needed in the American classroom is "one that is glowing with positive energy and a love and appreciation of people, is curious, wants to know, and enjoys sharing the excitement about a new idea or concept with other people."

Gloria Anderson of Virginia drives home this point when she comments that many capable students do not "have the appropriate levels of tolerance and patience necessary to become outstanding teachers. At least as important as having exceptional ability and knowledge of the subject matter is the ability to humanize instruc-

*D*oes it really take a Ph.D. from Harvard to teach math to 12-year-olds?

tion and to deliver it at the developmentally appropriate level for each child."

So, to be effective, teachers need not be full-fledged Einsteins spouting complex equations or eloquent conversationalists always ready with an apt quote from Shakespeare, but they do have to have some mastery of some subject matter. What do they need to know, and at what level of expertise? To a large degree, that depends on the grade or level they teach. In-depth knowledge of a specific subject is generally more important at the secondary level than the elementary level. High school teaching has traditionally been subject oriented, elementary teaching has been more child centered, and instruction at the middle level serves as a bridge between the two.

This delineation can be seen clearly when teachers from different grade levels discuss the importance of a mastery of subject matter. Anne Neidhardt thinks that high school science teachers such as herself should have a "really good knowledge of the content they're going to teach." She strongly recommends that all teachers on this level earn a master's degree in their area of concentration, be it chemistry, mathematics, or history. "Don't ever let anyone tell you," she says, "that you're over-educated for teaching. The more you know, the richer the fabric you bring to your classes. The more questions you can answer, the more innovative you can be. You add a richness that's not there if you don't know the content."

Judy Crawford is New Mexico's Teacher of the Year. She has been an elementary school teacher for nineteen years, and her perspective leads her to feel that "Teachers, as generalists, must have a broad knowledge of and curiosity about the world that allows them to identify and utilize resources that improve and enrich the curriculum. . . . The learning environment must evolve along with the development of the child and be centered around the interests of the child."

By contrast, Roberta Ford of Colorado teaches seventh grade. She recalls the early days of her twenty-two years of teaching: "Sub-

Their search for excellence often leads teachers to take risks.

ject matter was my forte . . . but, after I had been in the classroom a while, my goals for students underwent a dramatic change. Academics were still important, however I began to see them not as an end in themselves but rather as a means of helping students learn more important lessons—the lessons of self-worth and living."

This is not to suggest that, to be effective, first- and second-grade teachers should be kindly caretakers and high school teachers subject-crazed storm troopers. On the other hand, it is undeniable that the academic preparation necessary for teaching algebra II successfully is more demanding than that required for teaching simple addition.

The point is, whatever the subject matter, the grade level, or the degree of training required, the best teachers are always learners themselves. Whether they teach kindergarten or Advanced Placement calculus, they are eager to participate actively in the learning process.

And how do they do this? They avoid stagnation at all costs, because it is intellectually crippling to students and to themselves. Yellowed, dog-eared notes are anathema to good teachers. They cannot increase their knowledge base by relying on what has worked in the past, and the children's needs will not be met. Good teachers are constant tinkerers, scrutinizing their lessons and methods, changing something here or adding what Len DeAngelis calls "a new spice" there, learning from past mistakes as well as past successes.

Their search for excellence often leads teachers to take risks. "Teaching on the edge" is what Jolanda Cannon of West Virginia calls this willingness to take chances in the pursuit of excellence. It means being willing to try new things and take different approaches to old problems in an attempt to enhance the quality of

Teachers as learners work hard to pass along the legacy of lifelong learning to their students.

instruction. It means not relying too heavily on the safety of the textbook. The book is only one source of instructional material for a teacher who is actively involved in the learning process. There are anecdotes, current readings, and teacher-made materials, either swiped or invented, that can be used to embellish and amplify lessons.

Sure, teachers should know their stuff. That's obvious. But this doesn't necessarily mean having an encyclopedic knowledge of a specific subject. Effective teachers don't have to be walking compendiums of facts and figures. They don't need a degree from a prestigious college, and they don't have to graduate at the top of the class. Indeed, one of the pitfalls of formal education is that it gives the impression that learning stops with the granting of the degree—"John Jones completed his education at such-and-such a college." No one ever really *has* an education in this final sense. One is always in the process of *acquiring* it.

In *Improving Schools from Within*, Roland Barth quotes an anonymous teacher who said, "Learning is not something like chicken pox, a childhood disease that makes you itch for a while and then leaves you immune for the rest of your life." So much that was learned yesterday—about science, teaching methods, childhood development, and many other subjects related to education—is not entirely true today, and some of the things we know today we will not accept tomorrow. The frontier of understanding should be expanding continually to reveal what is new and correct what is old. The best teachers are met on that frontier with a powerful desire to serve the needs of kids.

128

Teachers as learners, the ones who populate America's best classrooms, work hard to pass along the legacy of lifelong learning to their students. Indiana's Mary Kay Baker shared with us her philosophy of teaching, which has nothing even remotely to do with chicken pox—"My philosophy has always included teaching children to love learning. I do not believe that one need be the brightest or best to love learning . . . I do believe that it is the responsibility of every teacher to instill in every student an understanding of the need for and the love of learning."

As Baker stepped back from her own classroom and viewed the broader landscape of education and society an additional thought came to her—"If *every* teacher tries to teach this to *every* child, public education will be successful in making this a better world. Achieve this goal, and lifelong learning is ensured."

Super Teacher . . .

- always hands back papers the very next day,
- never in his/her life has taken a sick day when he/she was not sick,
- never in his/her life has taken a sick day when he/she was sick.

Super Teacher . . .
- never doodles during faculty meetings,
- never dumps district communications into a file folder labeled "junk,"
- never forgets bus duty, not even accidentally.

Super Teacher . . .
- appreciates the instant and frequent communication offered by the intercom system,
- raises all window shades to the exact same height every afternoon before leaving school,
- never complains if he or she doesn't have windows.

Super Teacher . . .
- doesn't sweat, not even in an unairconditioned, 108° classroom,
- never gets blue ditto stains under his or her fingernails,
- never walks around with a streak of chalk dust on his or her behind.

Super Teacher . . .
- appreciates whatever the school board sees fit to pay,
- welcomes the challenge of having 37 kids in a class,
- schedules necessary surgery for spring break so he/she won't have to miss any school.

Super Teacher . . .
- has great respect for fire drills, even when held at lunchtime during a blizzard,
- never loses a child on the way to assembly,
- never has to go to the bathroom, except during the planning period.

Super Teacher . . .
- loves the school spirit generated by "Grubby Days," or "Dress Backwards Day,"
- never creates a new bulletin board by just slapping up a free poster,
- volunteers to be cheerleading sponsor every year.

Super Teacher . . .
- loves being observed and evaluated by the principal, appreciating the valuable criticism,
- never lectures students about "not thinking," or "setting an example," or "growing up,"
- doesn't exist in real life.

Excerpt from "Super Teacher" by Cheryl Miller Thurston (*Cottonwood Monthly*, January 1989). Copyright © 1988. Reprinted by permission of Cottonwood Press, Inc.

Afterword

Excellence comes in many different sizes and shapes. We have used stories, quotations, expert opinions, and research findings to describe a broad set of characteristics that distinguish excellence from mediocrity in the classroom. But excellence also occurs in small slices, hundreds and perhaps thousands of which make up a school day. On the facing page is a short list of recommendations for such mundane aspects of educational life as bus duty and fire drills.

Of course, the Super Teacher described there does not exist. The portrait is a composite. No teacher can turn pebbles into gold, spin plates, and still refrain from doodling in faculty meetings, and no teachers possess all the qualities delineated in this book (although many of the people we interviewed came real close). Our book, then, is not about perfection. It is not a checklist for entry into the Education Hall of Fame, nor is it the seven-step program to truth and enlightenment. It is simply a book about the grand promise within every person who decides to work with kids.

We also need to emphasize that teachers are only half of the education equation. Successful teachers usually come from successful schools, places that support, honor, and value learning. And successful schools are the joint product of their community, the school administration, and the teachers. Many people give teaching a try but leave before they've managed to develop their potential, often because of a bad initial experience. This is usually the fault of the school district, the school board, and the administrators.

How can a person tell the difference between schools that nurture teachers and those that grind them up and spit them out? A simple principle is to beware of schools or systems with high turnover rates of teachers and administrators. Good people have options in their professional lives, so when the situation becomes rotten they just leave. But the status quo also can be deceptive, because it can mask apathy and a lack of fresh ideas. An upmarket location or manicured lawns and eye-catching facilities are no gauge; they sometimes disguise serious, deep-rooted problems. Excellent schools exist in all sorts of places—in conservative, rural Winchester, New Hampshire, where exciting things are going on at Thayer High, or deep in the Chicago inner-city at Alexandre Dumas Elementary School, or in Corpus Christi, Texas, where principal Maggie Ramirez and her staff have turned the exclusively Mexican-American Lozano Special Emphasis School into a dynamic, vibrant institution where the daily attendance rate approaches 100 percent.

We think that a good school is much like a successful sports franchise. It has supportive, enthusiastic fans (parents and community), good coaches (administrators), and talented players (teachers). Seldom do players reach their full potential under poor management and coaching or without fan encouragement.

One last point. The teachers we interviewed have been on the job for many years. They didn't get this good overnight. Some had very rough starts, and some considered leaving. We think Wisconsin's Lee Schmitt said it about as candidly as it can be said when he told us, "No matter how much training you've had, and no matter how good you think you are and how much you've studied and know the material, *the first years are lousy.* You are doing a terrible job." After reflecting a moment, he went on to remark, "I can look back now and say that I was probably a very good teacher to the top 10 percent of my students, because I covered the content and

> **"No** *matter how much training you've had, and no matter how good you think you are, the first years are lousy.***"**

paged through the books, and I gave them lectures. I was 'unconsciously incompetent.' In other words, I was doing a bad job and didn't even know it."

Having described his initial brush with incompetence, Lee filled in the intervening years for us. "Later on, I became 'consciously incompetent.' I knew I wasn't doing as well as I could, but I didn't know why. With experience, a teacher becomes 'unconsciously competent.' That is, I became pretty good at teaching science, and the kids liked it. I was getting better, I was trying new experiments, developing new techniques, keeping the good, getting rid of the bad. That all comes with time.

"Well, I went back to school and studied education," he continued, "and began to learn a great deal more about the students I was teaching. I learned why certain things were working and others weren't. So here I am, after 15 years of teaching, and now I finally feel 'consciously competent.' I know what works, and I know why it works. And I can use that knowledge to improve my teaching even more."

It's a pretty simple recipe when you think of it: take a school system and community that value and support learning; blend in competent administrators; add a healthy splash of good teachers who aspire to be better; then give the ingredients time to mix and mature—a student at a time, a class at a time, a year at a time. The result? An eight-course educational banquet, from hors d'oeuvres to dessert—America's best classrooms.

Bibliography

American Association of School Administrators. *Challenges for School Leaders.* Arlington, Va.: American Association of School Administrators, 1988.

Barth, Roland. *Improving Schools from Within.* San Francisco: Jossey-Bass, 1990.

Boyer, Ernest. *High School.* New York: Harper & Row, 1983.

Cheney, Lynne. *Tyrannical Machines: A Report on Educational Practices Gone Wrong and Our Best Hopes for Setting Them Right.* Washington, D.C.: National Endowment for the Humanities, 1990.

Coles, Robert. *Instructor,* September 1990, pp. 58–59.

Cooperative Learning: Theory and Research. New York: Praeger, 1989.

Demmon-Berger, Debbie. *Effective Teaching: Observations from Research.* Arlington, Va.: American Association of School Administrators, 1986.

Feistritzer, C. Emily. *Profile of Teachers in the U.S.—1990.* Washington, D.C.: National Center for Education Information, 1990.

Foot, Hugh, et al. *Children Helping Children.* New York: Wiley, 1989.

Ginott, Hiam. *Teacher and Child.* New York: Macmillan, 1972.

Goodlad, John. *A Place Called School.* New York: McGraw-Hill, 1984.

———. *Teachers for Our Nation's Schools.* San Francisco: Jossey-Bass, 1990.

Handbook of Research on Teacher Education. New York: Macmillan, 1990.

Henderson, Anne. *The Evidence Continues to Grow: Parent Involvement Improves Student Achievement.* Columbia, Md.: National Committee for Citizens in Education, 1987.

Jorde, Paula. *Avoiding Burnout: Strategies for Managing Time, Space, and People in Early Childhood Education.* Washington, D.C.: Acropolis, 1982.

Kidder, Tracy. *Among Schoolchildren.* Boston: Houghton Mifflin, 1989.

Kohl, Herbert. *Growing Minds: On Becoming a Teacher.* New York: Harper & Row, 1984.

Lortie, Daniel. *Schoolteacher.* Chicago: University of Chicago Press, 1975.

Maeroff, Gene. *Voices from the Classroom: Exceptional Teachers Speak.* Washington, D.C.: National Foundation for the Improvement of Education, 1990.

Magid, Ken, and Carole A. McKelvey. *High Risk.* Golden, Colo.: M & M Publishing, 1987.

Mullis, Ina, Eugene Owen, and Gary Phillips, eds. National Center for Education Statistics. *Accelerating Academic Achievement.* Princeton, N.J.: Educational Testing Service, 1990.

Murray, Frank, and Daniel Fallon. *The Reform of Teacher Education for the 21st Century: Project 30 Year One Report.* Newark, Del.: Project 30, 1989.

A Nation at Risk: The Full Account. Boston: USA Research, 1984.

National Assessment of Educational Progress. *Nation's Report Card.* Princeton, N.J.: Educational Testing Service, 1990.

The National PTA Talks to Parents. New York: Doubleday, 1989.

Roueche, John, and George Baker. *Profiling Excellence in America's Schools.* Arlington, Va.: American Association of School Administrators, 1986.

Steuteville-Brodinsky, Mary, Russ Brodinsky, and Charles Harrison. *Excellent Teachers: Selecting, Recruiting, and Keeping.* Arlington, Va.: American Association of School Administrators, 1989.

Time for Results: The Governors' 1991 Report on Education. Washington, D.C.: National Governors' Association, 1986.

Tomorrow's Schools: Principles for the Design of Professional Development Schools. East Lansing, Mich.: The Holmes Group, 1990.

Tomorrow's Teachers: A Report of the Holmes Group. East Lansing, Mich.: The Holmes Group, 1986.

Wlodkowski, Raymond, and Judith Jaynes. *Eager to Learn.* San Francisco: Jossey-Bass, 1990.